'Richthofen's Circu

Jagdgeschwader Nr 1

Aviation Elite Units • 16

'Richthofen's Circus'

Jagdgeschwader Nr 1

Greg VanWyngarden

Series editor Tony Holmes

Front Cover

On the morning of 12 March 1918, nine Bristol F 2B Fighters of No 62 Sqn, Royal Flying Corps (RFC), were intercepted by a flight of Fokker Dr Is of *Jasta* 11, the premier unit of *Jagdgeschwader* (JG) I, near Le Cateau. The triplanes were led by none other than Manfred von Richthofen in Dr I 152/17, accompanied by his brother Lothar in Dr I 454/17 and Ltn Werner Steinhäuser. At 1100 hrs the Fokkers stabbed into the formation of Bristols. After watching his brother bring down one of the two-seaters, Lothar looked around for an opponent of his own;

'To that end there was one especially suited for me about 100 metres below the English squadron. I attacked him. I was flying ahead of my *Staffel* when I suddenly saw that I was surrounded by aircraft with English cockades. I made a long dive of about 100 metres in order to get out of that unpleasant company. One of them followed me down. At the same altitude, we flew toward one another, head-on. We approached each other with the great speed of over 400 km/h. Here, you must aim clean, otherwise you will get the worst of it.

'We rushed towards one another shooting. At the last moment I noticed I had hit him. A blazing aircraft whizzed by me. I pulled my machine around and made such a sharp turn that I was three-quarters on my back. A sea of fire in the form of an Englishman whistled right by me. The observer stood up and stared into the flames. Completely ablaze, the English machine made another turn. Both crewmen jumped out along the way.'

In the running battle that followed, Lothar brought down another Bristol ten minutes later, and Steinhäuser added one more to bring his personal tally to four. These victories contributed to a total of seven for the day by JG I, the most legendary of all German fighter units of World War 1 (*Cover artwork by Mark Postlethwaite*)

First published in Great Britain in 2004 by Osprey Publishing
1st Floor, Elms Court, Chapel Way, Botley, Oxford, OX2 9LP

© 2004 Osprey Publishing Limited

ISBN 1 84176 726 3

Edited by Tony Holmes
Page design by Mark Holt
Cover Artwork by Mark Postlethwaite
Aircraft Profiles by Harry Dempsey
Index by Alan Thatcher
Origination by Grasmere Digital Imaging, Leeds, UK
Printed in Hong Kong through Bookbuilders

04 05 06 07 08   10 9 8 7 6 5 4 3 2 1

ACKNOWLEDGEMENTS

The author wishes to thank R Duiven, P M Grosz, A Weaver, L Bronnenkant, G H Williams, S T Lawson, Dr G Merrill, D S Abbott, Suzanne Hayes Fischer, P S Leaman, R Rimell, Dave Roberts, Gunnar Söderbaum, Jörn Leckschied, Dr Dieter H M Gröschel, Dr D Gavish, D Watts, F Olynyk, N Franks, F Bailey, R Kastner and so many others who helped in the compilation of this work. The advice, photos and information provided by Alex Imrie were of great value. The respected historian Manfred Thiemeyer gave several valuable insights. Wouter Warmoes generously provided valuable photos. Thanks are extended to Peter Kilduff, an acknowledged expert on Richthofen and JG I, for his assistance and the inspiration and information provided by his books, all of which are recommended. The staff of the History of Aviation Collection at the University of Texas, in Dallas, were always very helpful. Finally, O'Brien Browne and Jan Hayzlett generously supplied many translations of German literature, making this book possible. Ms Hayzlett's translation of *Jagd in Flanderns Himmel* is priceless for those who wish to pursue the original source material.

CONTENTS

ORIGINS AND FORMATION

ermany's most famous flying formation of World War 1 came into being on 24 June 1917. As the first fighter wing in the *Luftstreitkräfte* (German Air Service), it would be known as *Jagdgeschwader* Nr I, or simply JG I. It was a permanent grouping of four existing *Jagdstaffeln* (*Jastas,* or 'hunting sections'), specifically *Jastas* 4, 6, 10 and 11 – thus it had a strength of some 50 aircraft.

The history of this unit is forever linked with that of its first and most successful commander, the celebrated Rittmeister Manfred Freiherr von Richthofen, then known as 'the red battle flier', and still world-famous as the 'Red Baron'. JG I was known as *'Geschwader* Richthofen' to most German airmen, and as 'Richthofen's Travelling Circus' by its foes of the RFC due to the unit's propensity for moving up and down the Front to wherever the fighting was most intense. After the Rittmeister's death in

The 'Ringmaster' of the 'Flying Circus' – Manfred Freiherr von Richthofen climbs into the cockpit of the Albatros D III he flew in early 1917. The aircraft's fuselage and tail unit were overpainted with a somewhat translucent coat of red, which partially obscured the fuselage cross. The serial number of this machine remains a mystery, the centrally-mounted radiator in the top wing indicating that it was an earlier number than D.2200/16, and thus not the D III D.789/17 he flew in June. Richthofen's bulky fur flying boots necessitated the use of the stepladder

combat following his 80th victory, the unit was officially redesignated *Jagdgeschwader* Freiherr von Richthofen Nr I by order of the Kaiser. After 16 months of aerial combat, the *Geschwader* was dissolved in November 1918, credited with 644 victories.

By the time JG I was formed in June 1917, aerial warfare had come a long way since its crude beginnings over two years earlier. In 1916 both sides had introduced single-seat fighters armed with machine guns. Foremost on the German side had been the famed Fokker Eindecker, or monoplane. Several pilots gained fame piloting the Eindecker, with the foremost of these being the great *Kanone* (ace) Oswald Boelcke, who also became Germany's first great aerial tactician and air combat leader. The Allied air forces eventually countered the Eindecker with nimble single-seaters like the French Nieuport 11 and British DH 2. The concept of 'aerial supremacy' was gradually forming, and the balance shifted to the Allies over the battlefields of Verdun and the Somme in mid-1916.

In an attempt to counter the Allied air superiority, the *Chef des Feldflugwesens* (Chief of Field Aviation) Maj Hermann von der Lieth-Thomsen ordered the formation of new dedicated single-seat fighting units – the *Jagdstaffeln* or *Jastas* – in August 1916, each *Jasta* having an official strength of 14 aeroplanes. The first seven *Jagdstaffeln* were created from existing groupings of fighters known as *Kampfeinsitzer Kommandos* (KEK).

Together with the introduction of new biplane fighters such as the excellent Albatros D I and D II, the *Jastas* would employ tactics developed by Boelcke to begin to regain control of the air. The cutting edge of this effort was Boelcke's own *Jasta* 2, flying its Albatros fighters in the fiercely contested skies over the Battle of the Somme. One of Boelcke's hand-picked pilots was Ltn Manfred Freiherr von Richthofen.

Under the watchful eye of his mentor Boelcke, Richthofen honed his hunter's stalking skills to become a deadly and proficient *Jagdflieger*. He was awarded the coveted *Orden Pour le Mérite* (the 'Blue Max') on 12 January 1917 following his 16th aerial triumph, and two days later he was given command of his own unit, *Jasta* 11. Under its previous commander, this *Jasta* had yet to score a single victory in three months at the Front. Richthofen, however, would change that.

JAGDSTAFFEL 11

Destined to become the highest scoring *Jasta* of the war, this unit was officially formed on 28 September 1916 and became operational under the command of Oblt Rudolf Lang on 11 October. It was based at Brayelles airfield near Douai, just east of Arras, on the German 6. *Armee* Front, and was equipped with Halberstadt biplanes. Richthofen arrived to take command on 16 January 1917, and wasted no time in infusing the men of his command with the offensive spirit of Boelcke. Richthofen was fortunate in that he enjoyed a good relationship with the *Kommandeur der Flieger (Kofl)* of the 6. *Armee*, Hptm Sorg.

By the third week of January Richthofen had obtained some of the new Albatros D IIIs for his pilots. The new CO led by example, downing an FE 8 on 23 January for the first victory of the *Staffel,* followed by another the next day. In February six more *Jasta* 11 victories were obtained, as the unit's airmen began to show the results of Richthofen's tutelage.

Kurt Wolff poses in an early photograph with a Halberstadt fighter – the type which equipped *Jasta* 11 before Richthofen took command. Wolff had not scored a single victory when Richthofen took over, but he would learn a great deal from the master's tutelage, and would make up for lost time in March and April 1917

Although slightly blurred, this photograph is important as it reveals *Jasta* 11 star Ltn Karl Emil Schäfer with his Albatros D III in the spring of 1917. There are several contemporary references which describe Schäfer's Albatros as yellow with a black tail. The 'yellow' would seem to have been simply bright varnished plywood, while the rear fuselage, tail, wheel covers and probably the nose were black – the wings retained their factory camouflage. This machine may have been repainted predominantly red some time in mid-April 1917. The scarf knotted in a buttonhole of Schäfer's coat was used for wiping the pilot's goggles in flight. While he played no actual role in JG I, Schäfer's victories of March and April contributed greatly to the record and legend of *Jasta* 11 (*HAC/UTD*)

Under his watchful guidance, some of his young hunters were transformed into superb fighter pilots. There was the frail-looking Ltn Kurt Wolff, just turned 22, a former railway transportation officer of humorous and shy demeanour. Ironically nicknamed *'zarte Blümlein'* ('delicate little blossom'), he would become Richthofen's close friend and most successful protégé. Fellow *Jasta* 11 tyro 20-year-old Ltn Karl Allmenröder had abandoned his medical studies to join the artillery, then transferred to aviation with his elder brother Wilhelm – both brothers wound up in *Jasta* 11 in September 1916. Another promising pilot was 22-year-old NCO Vzfw Sebastian Festner. On 5 February 1917, the tall, slender Ltn d R Karl Emil Schäfer reported to the *Staffel*, having written directly to Richthofen after scoring his first kill in *Kampfstaffel* 11. The 25-year-old had been slightly lamed by a wound during his infantry service, but he showed the aggressive spirit the *Jasta* 11 CO looked for.

Manfred von Richthofen welcomed a familiar face to the *Jasta* on 10 March when his brother Lothar arrived. Two years younger than his famous sibling, he was posted to *Jasta* 11 following flight training, having served as an observer. Lothar wasted no time in emulating his brother, scoring his first victory that same month.

Indeed, March was a successful month for *Jasta* 11, and a portent of things to come. As British forces prepared for the Battle of Arras, the tempo of aerial activity around Douai intensified, and *Jasta* 11 met the challenge superbly under the newly-promoted Oblt von Richthofen. Some 27 British aircraft fell to the guns of the *Staffel* in March, ten of them claimed by the commander. His 'pups' were gaining deadly skill themselves – Schäfer claimed seven victories that month, Wolff had five, and Allmenröder gained three. *Jasta* 11 outscored every other *Staffel* in the German air service in March 1917, and all this was achieved despite troubling problems with failures of the Albatros D III's lower wings, which temporarily grounded the type.

The British offensive known as the Battle of Arras technically began on 9 April, but the aerial offensive had commenced five days earlier as the RFC attempted to drive German aircraft away from the battle front so their own crews could operate without interference.

The British First and Third Armies had amassed some 365 operational aircraft on the Arras Front, split between 25 squadrons. At the outset,

these were opposed by 195 German aircraft of the 6. *Armee*. Besides *Jasta* 11 there were seven other fighter *Staffeln* operating on the Arras Front, but due to attrition and replacement problems, most of these formations had an average daily strength of only seven aircraft. For the first 12 days of April there were, daily, only about 42 fighter aircraft available for action – a figure which increased to 56 by the end of the month.

The pilots of *Jasta* 11 were not intimated by the odds against them. They had now been forged into a formidable, experienced and eager combat team, and they found themselves in what today would be called a 'target-rich environment'. The weeks that followed would be grimly remembered as 'Bloody April' by the RFC. Repeatedly sent out over the lines, usually in inferior aircraft, the courageous British airmen suffered grievous casualties. It was a time of terrific effort by the *Jagdstaffeln,* and the units achieved great results, but suffered significant losses themselves.

Leading the way in the carnage was *Jasta* 11, the most successful *Staffel* with 89 confirmed April victories. Richthofen himself attained 21 kills that month, in the process surpassing the score of his idol Boelcke and being promoted to Rittmeister. His friend Wolff shot down 23, while Schäfer and Lothar each downed 15 British machines. Allmenröder brought his score to nine, and the modest Bavarian Festner had raised his tally to 12 by the time he was killed in action on the 25th.

Jagdstaffel 11 had reached legendary status amongst the German troops and general public by the end of the heady month of April. Much of the mystique surrounding the unit is derived from its leadership by the 'Red Knight' and the colourful aircraft flown by the unit. Richthofen's use of red as an identifying colour began in *Jasta* 2, where it was discovered that the reddish-brown paint intended to camouflage the Albatros fighters ironically made the machines *more* visible. The *Jagdflieger* placed great importance on the ability to be recognised in the air – both for the

Another early star of *Jasta* 11 was Karl Allmenröder, seen here in this view from late June 1917 on the right, with Oblt Hans von Boddien at left. Allmenröder's Albatros D III (D.629/17) bore classic *Jasta* 11 markings for this period – a red fuselage, struts and tail, with some distinguishing trim in another colour for individual identification. Allmenröder's personal colour was white, displayed on the nose and elevator – again the camouflage on the wings remained untouched. The considerable wear visible on the fuselage beneath the cockpit resulted from the use of a stepladder for the pilot, and shows this machine had been in use for awhile

MANFRED VON RICHTHOFEN

The most successful fighter pilot of World War 1 was born on 2 May 1892 in the Lower Silesian town of Kleinberg, near Schweidnitz. His father was a retired career Army officer, and Manfred was destined to follow in his father's footsteps – he entered the Cadet Institute at Wahlstatt at the age of 11. He graduated to the Main Cadet Institute at Gross-Lichterfelde in 1909, and was commissioned as a leutnant in the Silesian *Ulanen-Regiment (Kaiser Alexander III von Russland)* Nr 1 in 1912. When the war began Richthofen's unit was sent to the Eastern Front, and he saw service both in Russia and then France. Dissatisfied with the inaction he experienced on the latter Front, he petitioned to transfer to the air service, which he did in May 1915.

After training as an observer Richthofen was sent back to the Eastern Front with *Fled-flieger Abteilung* 69, then served with *Brieftauben Abteilung Ostende (BAO)* – a cover name for a multi-task unit which operated over the Flanders Front. After a chance meeting with Boelcke, he was inspired to pursue fighter pilot training, and completed this in December 1915. While serving as a pilot with *Kampfgeschwader* 2 in Russia, Richthofen was tapped for Boelcke's new *Jasta* 2. Flying the Albatros D II, Richthofen rewarded Boelcke's faith in him by downing an FE 2b on 17 September 1916 – the momentous first

of an eventual 80 kills. After Boelcke's death on 28 October, Richthofen really showed his promise when he downed the DH 2 of Maj Lanoe G Hawker, the CO of No 24 Sqn and Britain's premier fighter tactician, on 23 November for his 11th victory.

On 10 January 1917 he was made commander of *Jasta* 11, and two days later received the news of his *Pour le Mérite*, which followed his 24th claim. As a *Staffelführer* Richthofen proved to be as skilful a leader, trainer and organiser as he was a fighter pilot. He rose to the rank of Rittmeister on 6 April.

By the end of 'Bloody April' Richthofen had surpassed his idol Boelcke's score with 53 victories, and his *Jasta* 11 was famous throughout Germany. It was only logical that he be given command of the first Fighter Wing in the *Luftstreitkräfte,* but his leadership of *Jagdgeschwader* Nr I was soon interrupted by his near-fatal head wound of 6 July.

Richthofen returned to combat far too soon, plagued by headaches and exhaustion after every flight. Nonetheless, his was a war of duty, and he persevered. Although many of his superiors and family urged him to retire from combat flying, he refused. In March and April 1918 he seemed to be back to his old form, scoring 16 kills in less than six weeks. His death on 21 April remains a subject of controversy, but his score would not be surpassed in World War 1, nor would his legend.

The first commander of *Jagdgeschwader* I, Rittmeister Manfred Freiherr von Richthofen is seen here convalescing on the porch at Chateau Marckebeeke after suffering a head wound in combat on 6 July 1917

coordination of formations and for confirmation of victories by ground observers.

Many reasons have been given for Richthofen's choice of red as his own décor, one being that this was the regimental colour of his old Uhlan regiment. It was undoubtedly simply the factor of recognition, though, that convinced Richthofen to have his Albatros D III painted red in January 1917. *Jasta* 11 subsequently implemented a policy wherein each pilot identified his own D III with a distinctive colour scheme.

On 3 March, Ltn Eduard Lübbert of the *Jasta* described the colours of the aircraft flown by some of his squadronmates – Freiherr von Richthofen had a 'bright red' (*knallrote*) machine, Schäfer's aircraft was 'yellow with a black tail', Kurt Wolff flew a 'purple plum' (*violette Pflaum*), Karl Allmenröder had a field grey (*feldgrau*) crate, while Lübbert himself flew a D III which was 'half blue, half yellow'.

On 11 April the German journalist *Prof Dr* Georg Wegener visited the famous unit at Brayelles, and left an evocative portrait of *Jasta* 11;

'At the edge of the open airfield, five biplanes stood in a row, ready for take-off; a sixth one – Freiherr von Richthofen's – was somewhat in front and off to the side . . . all were differently painted. From a distance, they looked like brightly coloured giant insects, like a swarm of radiant butterflies which were sunning themselves on the ground with wings spread wide. The principle of looking as much as possible like the colour of the sky was totally abandoned. Invisibility, it was explained to me, one cannot obtain. Indeed one runs the danger of confusing enemy and friendly aircraft. These different markings on the fuselages are clearly visible in the air, and one recognises the others in a fight and can support them.

Like his mentor Richthofen (whose portrait is seen in front of the bookshelf), Kurt Wolff was an avid collector of serial number fabric pieces from his victims. In the background are souvenirs from FE 2b 7691, downed on 31 March 1917, and Bristol F 2B Fighter A3338 claimed on 11 April (*HAC/UTD*)

It was recorded on 3 March 1917 that Kurt Wolff flew a 'plum purple' Albatros D III, and it has been suggested that the machine (D.632/17) seen here with Wolff was this aircraft. However, this particular D III did not arrive at *Jasta* 11 until 19 April 1917. The author believes that D.632/17 bore the red finish common to many of the *Staffel* 11 machines by mid-April, as the national insignia clearly provide evidence of overpainting in the usual style. Lothar von Richthofen wrote that Wolff flew a red Albatros with green trim – perhaps the spinner and elevator of this D III were green? Note that the serial number was still legible through the thin coat of paint (*P Kilduff*)

'This is why each pilot has his personal machine which he always flies, and with which he grows close to as with a living creature – it is given a special marking which allows his comrades to keep an eye on him during a fight, and to always know who is flying this aircraft. One machine has a white or red or another coloured stripe, another wore this diagonally or straight or so on. From Richthofen's eyes shine something like the pride of a warrior knight who knows that his shield and helmet ornament are known and feared by his opponent. "I make sure that my squadron sees me wherever I am".'

Clearly, many of the fighters of *Jasta* 11 were brightly coloured, but the Rittmeister's red Albatros still stood out. Interrogations of captured airmen made it clear that it was well known to the RFC, and the men of *Jasta* 11 were very concerned that a trap would be planned for its pilot. As a result, many of the *Jasta's* Albatros D IIIs were painted largely red by mid-April, possibly after the unit's move to Roucourt airfield on the 16th. By the 30th, Ltn Carl Bauer of neighbouring *Jasta* 3 recorded the popular (but erroneous) belief that, 'the English had put a price on Richthofen's head, with the stipulation that the red machine is shot down. As a consequence Richthofen now has all machines of his *Staffel* painted red'.

After the war, Lothar von Richthofen would write (translated by Peter Kilduff);

'It had long been our wish to have all aeroplanes of our *Staffel* painted red, and we implored my brother to allow it. The request was granted, for

Unfortunately the circumstances and location of this interesting photo of Richthofen's red Albatros D III are unknown, as is the reason for the detached aileron cables. The machine appears to be in pristine condition, although without its elevator. The factory finish camouflage is still visible on the drooping ailerons. Note the small unpainted rectangle for the Albatros company crest on the rudder (*Courtesy Lance Bronnenkant*)

Two Albatros D Vs head this line-up of *Jasta* 11 D IIIs at Roucourt in late May or early June 1917. The first five aircraft at least seem to have been largely painted red. The foremost D V has an 'individual' fuselage band in another colour. The third scout (a D III) bore overpainted national insignia on the fuselage and tail, and may have been one of Richthofen's aircraft (*HAC/UTD*)

A pilot reported to be Lothar von Richthofen sits in new Albatros D V D.1100/17 as the engine is prepared for starting. This aircraft came from the first production batch of 200 ordered in April 1917, and may have just arrived. It as yet bore no special markings, but was fitted with the high headrest characteristic of early D Vs. The pilots complained that this headrest obstructed their view aft, and most were removed in service (*HAC/UTD*)

we had shown ourselves worthy of the red colour by our many aerial kills. The red colour signified a certain insolence. Everyone knew that. It attracted attention. Proudly, we looked at our red birds. My brother's crate was glaring red. Each of the rest of us had some additional markings in other colours – we chose these colours as recognition symbols. Schäfer, for example, had his elevator, rudder and most of the back part of the fuselage painted black, Allmenröder used white, Wolff used green and I had yellow. As a yellow dragooneer, that was the appropriate colour for me.

'In the air and from the ground, as well as from the enemy's view, we all looked to be red, as only small parts were painted in another colour.'

Lothar's description is understandably vague, but it gives a fair impression of the appearance of *Jasta* 11 aircraft at this time. The red was generally applied to the fuselage, tail, struts and wheel covers, and often applied as a translucent 'wash' over the national insignia and serial.

As 'Bloody April' ground inexorably to its end, both sides tried out new tactics. As the formations of RFC aircraft became larger and better coordinated, the Germans responded in fashion. On 30 April fighters from *Jastas* 3, 4, 11 and 33 were combined into one large group. They sortied 20 fighters in two formations, which made general sweeps from Douai behind the battle area. The massed use of fighters in this way was a prototype of the *Jagdgeschwader* operations to come. *Jasta* 11 was led on this day by Lothar, who downed two aircraft. Manfred would soon go on leave after his spectacular success on the 29th, when he downed four in one day to bring his score to 52.

With better British aircraft like the SE 5, DH 4, and Bristol F 2B Fighter arriving, the momentum achieved by *Jasta* 11 began to fade. The unit would down a very respectable 28 opponents in May, but suffered four casualties.

The redoubtable Karl Emil Schäfer, victor over 23 British machines, was appointed commander of *Jasta* 28 on 26 April (he would fall in battle on 5 June). Richthofen's iron band of deadly hunters was beginning to be split up. The veteran Kurt Wolff was awarded the *Pour le Mérite* on 4 May, but six days later was appointed commander of *Jasta* 29 to replace its fallen leader. Lothar himself was wounded by ground fire on the fateful 13th day of the month – an unlucky number that would continue to bedevil him. Allmenröder took temporary command of the *Staffel*, and it was in May that he would really hit his stride. He was the star of the *Jasta* that month, scoring 13 victories to raise his total to 22. Allmenröder went on to add eight more in June and win his own *Pour le Mérite* on the 14th, with his score at 26.

In June, the dismal failure of the French Nivelle Offensive on the Aisne led to the transfer of effort to the British Front in Flanders. The intention of the Flanders offensives was to clear the Belgian coast of German forces, bringing pressure to bear on the northern flank of their defences. The Battles of Messines Ridge (which began on 7 June) and the Third Battle of Ypres (31 July) brought intense RFC activity against the German 4. *Armee*. *Jasta* 11 was one of several units relocated to the north to counter this threat, and on 10 June the *Staffel* completed a move from Roucourt to Harlebeke-Bavichove on the 4. *Armee* front.

The Rittmeister had returned from leave in early June, and on the 18th he downed an RE 8 for his 53rd victory, and the 163rd for *Jasta* 11. He had brought his personal tally to an unprecedented 55 by the 24th – the day of the official formation of *Jagdgeschwader* I. The next day Richthofen was officially informed by telegram that he would be the commander of this new wing, and he celebrated by shooting down an RE 8. This patrol was led by Allmenröder, who was now full-time commander of *Jasta* 11.

On 26 June *Jagdgeschwader* I received its charter from the *Kommandierenden General der Luftstreitkräfte (Kogenluft)*, Gen von Höppner, in a telegram. With military efficiency, it read simply;

'*Jagdgeschwader* Nr I comprises *Jasta* 4,6,10 and 11. The *Geschwader* is a self-contained unit. Duty is to attain and maintain air supremacy in sectors of the Front as directed.'

Richthofen was now in command of a mobile unit that was capable of putting up 50 to 60 fighters in a combat area. The reasons for these new tactics were explained by the last commander of JG I, Hermann Göring, who wrote;

On 4 June 1917 Ltn Georg Simon of *Jasta* 11 was shot down by Capt Chapman of No 29 Sqn RFC and taken prisoner. He brought down his D III (D.2015/16) intact behind British lines, and it became the subject of technical reports and was test flown by various British pilots. The fighter displayed classic *Jasta* 11 markings for late spring 1917, for its fuselage, tail, struts and undercarriage were painted 'bright red, which is either vermilion with crimson lake or geranium lake only'. The fuselage band aft of the cockpit was green, composed of 'common Brunswick green and white'. Seen here with British markings, it probably originally had its German national insignia obscured by a translucent coat of red like other *Jasta* 11 D IIIs

'It was apparent that the Englishmen often simultaneously appeared with over 50 aircraft during the aerial battles in Flanders, and we could not oppose such a mass with any combat group led in a unified manner in the appropriate strength. Secondly, there originated in the person of Rittmeister Freiherr von Richthofen a fighter pilot whose excellent, wide-ranging leadership skills had to be put to better use than what was possible at the level of a *Jagdstaffel*. The purpose of this *Jagdgeschwader* was to deploy it to the hot points of the major embattled areas of the Front in order to break enemy aerial superiority there, and to secure command of the air for our own working aircraft.'

Before *Geschwader* operations could really get started, *Jasta* 11 suffered yet another crippling loss. On 27 June *Staffelführer* Karl Allmenröder fell in pursuit of his 31st victory. The well-known story that he was shot down by Canadian ace Raymond Collishaw of 10 Naval Squadron, RNAS, does not stand up to close scrutiny.

The 21-year-old Rhinelander was killed in the morning, and Collishaw's action took place in the evening. A German eyewitness account published in 1938 indicated that the ace's Albatros was downed by ground fire while returning low over the lines. *Jasta* 11 was suddenly leaderless at this critical time. Richthofen succeeded in having his friend Kurt Wolff transferred from the command of *Jasta 29* in order to take over his old *Staffel*. He could hardly have made a better choice, and no doubt welcomed his comrade warmly, knowing that his cherished *Jasta* 11 would be in good hands. But what of the other three units in JG I?

JAGDSTAFFEL 4

On 25 August 1916, *Jasta* 4 had been created around the formation known as KEK Vaux, which was a unit with several celebrated aces. It would be first based at Vaux, then Roupy, in the German 2. *Armee* sector, and was initially equipped with Halberstadt D types. The formation of *Jasta* 4 was handled by a veteran of KEK Vaux, the legendary

Richthofen paid a visit to the base of *Kagohl* 3 at Gontrode in the summer of 1917, and he is seen here with KG 3 commander Oblt Rudolf Kleine at left, with his adjutant Oblt Gerlich in the middle. Visible in the background are the Albatros D Vs flown by Richthofen and another unknown *Jasta* 11 pilot. It is the author's belief that this photograph was taken circa June 1917, prior to Richthofen being shot down, as there is certainly no visible evidence of his head wound here

iron-willed ace Rudolf Berthold, but on 1 September he handed the command of the unit to Oblt Hans-Joachim Buddecke – the latter was already a *Pour le Mérite* holder, as was another *Jasta* 4 pilot, Ltn d R Wilhelm Frankl. The early roster of *Jasta* 4 would include such worthies as Bernert, Frankl, von Althaus and Berthold. Ltn Otto Bernert scored first blood for *Jasta* 4 on 6 September when he downed a French Caudron. He would bring his total to seven in two months in *Jasta* 4, but would then transfer to *Jasta* Boelcke (and briefly serve as commander of *Jasta* 6).

In September alone, at least 12 confirmed enemy aircraft fell to the guns of the Halberstadt pilots of *Jasta* 4, along with eight unconfirmed and one 'forced to land'. Besides Bernert and the hard-charging Berthold, the obvious 'star' of the *Staffel* in these days was Frankl, another KEK Vaux ace from the 'Fokker scourge' era. On 12 July 1916, after eight kills, he had become the only Jewish *Pour le Mérite* winner of the air service. Frankl added four victories in September, with Berthold and Bernert each adding two of their own. In October, Frankl scored half of the unit's four victories.

In November the fortunes of the *Staffel* continued to ebb, with only three aircraft downed – all by Bernert. In December, Buddecke was sent to the Turkish Front and the *Jasta* was transferred to Hivry-Circourt in the 5. *Armee* sector near Verdun. It is believed that acting leadership of the *Jasta* was given to Frankl for about two months, after which full command went to Oblt Kurt-Bertram von Döring, a 28-year-old ex-Mecklenburg Dragoon officer who had transferred to aviation in 1913. Döring had become one of Germany's few pre-war military pilots in 1914, and thus had a long career in the air service before taking command of *Jasta* 4.

In late February the *Jasta* was sent to Douai in the 6. *Armee* sector. With the arrival of Albatros D IIIs and 'Bloody April', the pace picked up, with 15 British aircraft and one balloon added to the *Jasta* 4 record books that grim month. Frankl was in fine form, downing four aircraft on the 6th, followed by another the succeeding day to bring his score to 20. On the 8th, however, he was attacking Bristol Fighters when his D III was seen to break up, and he fell to his death near Vitry-Sailly.

New pilots soon filled the void left by Frankl's demise. A future JG I star who began to make his mark was 26-year-old Ltn d R Hans Klein. He had seen intense infantry action in 1914-15, and won rapid promotion. He transferred to aviation at the end of 1915, and was posted to *Jasta* 4 on 4 November 1916. Klein was a man of small stature ('klein' is, ironically, German for 'little'), but he would play a big role in the JG I story.

Klein opened his account on 4 April by downing a hapless BE 2 near Arras. His second kill was a balloon three days later, with an FE 2 falling on the 5th. He achieved 'doubles' over two-seaters on the 11th and 13th, and closed out the month by bagging another BE 2 on the 30th. May saw Klein score one of only two victories claimed by his *Jasta*.

Jagdstaffel **4 commander Oblt Kurt-Bertram von Döring is seen here at left, holding a tight leash on the** *Staffel* **mascots named Spad, Vickers and Nieuport. At extreme right is** *Jasta* **4 pilot Hans Klein, a future** *Pour le Mérite* **winner and** *Jasta* **10 commander, with another pup. The Albatros D Vs show off the** *Jasta* **4 unit markings of a black ribbon wrapped around the fuselage in a spiral. Each aircraft was probably identified by a differently coloured spinner and tail**

The pilots of *Jasta* 4 pose for a more formal portrait, with the *Staffel* pets in evidence as usual. They are, standing, from left to right, unknown, Vfw Ernst Clausnitzer, unknown, *Staffelführer* Oblt von Döring, Vfw Linus Patermann, Ltn Busso von Alvensleben, unknown, and Ltn Wilhelm Schulze. Seated, from left to right, are unknown, Ltn Hans Klein in the centre with the dog and, his face blurred as he reacts to his frisky pup, future 'Blue Max' winner Ltn d R Kurt Wüsthoff. The Albatros aircraft in the background display the *Jasta* 4 wound ribbon unit markings. Note the two-tone spinner on the nearest aircraft

In June Klein's victory skein would continue, as he claimed an RE 8 and two more balloons. June also saw the first entry in the lists of another name that would figure prominently in the epic of the Richthofen *Geschwader* – 19-year-old Vfw Kurt Wüsthoff (born on 27 January 1898). This ambitious and aggressive youngster shot down a Sopwith $1^1/2$ Strutter on the 15th for his first success, and wrote to his mother the next day;

'Life is just brilliant here – more dangerous, mind you, as all hell has broken loose in the air and on the ground! We fly three to four times over the Front daily, with, of course, aerial fights each time. This morning I had an English single-seat fighter sitting right in front of me, who unfortunately chickened out too quickly. Well, still more will come. I hope to shoot down some alone soon because it is boring (flying) with others!'

Thus *Jasta* 4 had a distinguished pedigree, a seasoned commander and a core of promising pilots in its ranks. By July it was equipped with Albatros D Vs adorned with the unit's marking of a black 'wound ribbon' or 'snake-line', wrapped in a spiral around the varnished plywood fuselage. Each pilot's own machine was identified by a tail and propeller spinner painted in a personal colour or pattern of colours, presenting a vivid display.

JAGDSTAFFEL 6

Jasta 6 was formed from *Fokkerstaffel* Sivry in the 5. *Armee* on 25 August 1916. It was still equipped with eight weary Fokker monoplanes at formation, and was commanded by Josef Wulff. The old Fokkers were returned to AFP 5 at the end of September, and the *Staffel* was relocated to Jametz, then to Ugny le Quipée in the 2. *Armee* sector on the Somme. It was also re-equipped with powerful new Albatros D I fighters, and later with D IIs.

One of the charter members of the *Jasta* was the irrepressible Vfw Carl Holler who, in civilian life, had been a professional guitar-playing folk singer. He was delighted with the Albatros D I, writing;

'Its rate of climb was excellent. Because of its heavy in-line engine, it had a tremendous diving speed, which gave us great advantage when attacking

Early on, *Jasta* 6 was equipped with Albatros D I and D II fighters identified with large numbers on the fuselage. The happy pilot seen with this D II is the always-smiling Vfw Carl Holler who, in peacetime, was a professional entertainer with the stage name Niels Sörensen. Holler was an early member of *Jasta* 6, and he would score two confirmed victories and another 'forced to land'

In June 1917 the professional soldier Oblt Eduard Dostler took over *Jasta* 6. He had been commissioned on 28 October 1912 and began the war in the 4th Pioneer Battalion of the Bavarian Army. He won many decorations, including the Bavarian Life Saving medal for rescuing two of his men from drowning in the Danube in August 1914. He had served with distinction in *Jagdstaffeln* 13 and 34b before his posting to *Jasta* 6, and he would prove to be one of the early stalwarts of JG I

the enemy flying below. Now we did not have to wait very long to obtain a few victories. In short order, one after another, two of my comrades obtained a victory.'

Indeed Vfw Kress shot down a French Morane on 20 October for the first entry in the *Jasta* gamebook, followed by Ltns Roland Nauck, Friedrich Mallinckrodt and *Staffelführer* Wulff. By 10 November the *Jasta* had six confirmed claims, but suffered its first loss on that day when Kress was shot down, possibly by the French ace Guynemer.

With the onset of harsher winter weather, the aerial efforts of *Jasta* 6 seemed to stagnate, as no confirmed victories were forthcoming in December or January for the loss of one pilot killed and another wounded. Holler got things going again by claiming a Caudron for his first confirmed victim on 11 February. In March the pace quickened as the unit was re-equipped with the Albatros D III and better weather arrived. Ltn d R Kurt Küppers scored the first of his eventual six victories on the 15th. Five days later the *Staffel* moved north to Aulnoye, and finished March with four confirmed claims.

In 'Bloody April', however, the *Jasta* ironically achieved not a single victory, while losing Nauck on the 8th. Commander Wulff was replaced at the end of April by Ltn Bernert from *Jasta* Boelcke, now a 24-victory *Kanone* with a newly-won *Pour le Mérite* at his throat. Bernert galvanised the pilots of *Jasta* 6 by superb example, knocking down two aircraft and a balloon in just seven days. Eight triumphs in all came to the *Staffel* in May, with Holler and Vfw Fritz Krebs each getting two.

In the next month Bernert was called back to *Jasta* Boelcke to take command, and the *Staffel* was extremely fortunate in his replacement – Bavarian Oblt Eduard Dostler, aged 25, who had scored his first aerial victory as a Roland C II pilot in Bavarian *Kampfstaffel* 36. This success got him posted to *Jasta* 13, then to the command of *Jasta* 34b on 20 February 1917. Here, he was victor over six French aircraft, bringing his personal score to eight before his posting to *Jasta* 6 on 11 June.

Soon after the formation of the *Geschwader*, Dostler succeeded in having his right-hand man from *Jasta* 34b transferred to *Jasta* 6 as well – fellow Bavarian Ltn d Landwehr Hans Adam. Married, and the father of two children, the 31-year-old Adam had as yet but two kills. Nonetheless, he and Dostler would form a deadly team, and great things were in store for them both.

Jasta 6 had 31 victories, a superb CO and a fine roster when it joined JG I. Its Albatros D IIIs and D Vs were identified by broad black and white zebra stripes, painted chordwise on the horizontal tail surfaces. This marking would remain a proud feature of *Jasta* 6 aircraft to war's end.

JAGDSTAFFEL 10

Jasta 10 was officially formed on 28 September 1916, but as a unit it actually existed some days earlier. It derived from KEK 3 at Douai (as well as other units) in the 6. *Armee,* and moved to Phalempin airfield, near Lille, on 25 September. The unit's equipment originally consisted of a motley collection of Fokker, Halberstadt and Albatros types. Initially, Oblt Ludwig Linck commanded the *Staffel,* which had commenced operations at Phalempin by 6 October.

Four days later, Linck attempted to gain the unit's first success when he attacked an FE 2b and brought it down at Vitry. However, he was only given credit for having forced it to land, which did not qualify as a full victory in the German air service. On 22 October the *Staffel* lost its CO when Linck was shot down in flames. The unit then transferred to Jametz airfield, near Stenay, in late October. Linck was eventually succeeded by Oblt Volkmann, who brought no better luck to the *Jasta.* In fact, the unit compiled a lacklustre record in its first five months, attaining only a few confirmed victories. In December it moved to Ancrevillers, and by this time it probably had a full complement of Albatros machines.

The 25 of March 1917 finally brought the first *Jasta* 10 kill for Vfw Paul Aue, who downed a Nieuport near Verdun. It was in fact the diminutive Saxon's second victory, his first having been scored as a pilot with *Kampfstaffel* 30 of KG 5. Paul Aue would remain a stalwart of *Jasta* 10 right up to war's end, scoring seven more times.

Albatros D V D.1119/17 provides an appropriate backdrop for a group of *Jasta* 10 pilots in this classic photograph taken about one month after the formation of JG I. They are, from left to right, Uffz Hermann Brettel, Vfw Bansmer(?), Vfw Adam Barth, Ltn Erich Offermann, *Staffelführer* Oblt Ernst Freiherr von Althaus (in his distinctive hussar uniform, with the 'Blue Max' at his throat), Ltn Max Kühn, Oblt Ernst Weigand (deputy commander, and later acting *Staffelführer*), Ltn von Bieber-Palubizki, future *Pour le Mérite* winner Ltn Erich Löwenhardt and Vfw Aloys Heldmann. At this time Löwenhardt was just another pilot in the *Staffel,* and he would not score his first victory until 14 August – one wonders if any of these airmen would have guessed he would become the third-highest scoring *jagdflieger* in the *Luftstreitkräfte*. Note the high headrest on this early D V

Another nascent ace in the *Jasta* ranks was Ltn d R Aloys Heldmann, who had already seen extensive service as a two-seater pilot in Serbia, Bulgaria and the Western Front. He forced one of the vaunted Sopwith Triplanes to land on 2 May, but would have to wait 20 more days before his first confirmed victory (an RE 8). Like Aue, Heldmann became a steady performer, part of the backbone of the unit. Also 'waiting in the wings' was an airman whose name would become inseparably linked with *Jasta* 10 – Ltn Erich Löwenhardt, who started off his incredible string of 54 victories by downing a balloon on 28 March 1917.

Volkmann left the unit at the end of 1916, and Oblt Rummelspacher became acting commander. On 21 June the *Pour le Mérite* ace Ltn d R Albert Dossenbach assumed command of *Jasta* 10, which was now based at Heule, near Courtrai, in the 4. *Armee* sector. The 26-year-old Dossenbach, from Baden, was a experienced *Jasta* CO, and he flamed a balloon on 27 June for his 16th victory. His time at *Jasta* 10, however, would be brief.

Of the four component *Staffeln*, *Jasta* 10 had the least impressive record thus far. Nonetheless, a handful of young pilots remained eager to prove themselves in their Albatros fighters, which were brightly marked with yellow noses, struts and wheel covers.

GESCHWADER OPERATIONS COMMENCE

The last days of June were a hectic time for Richthofen, as he directed the movement of the four *Jagdstaffeln* to their new locations near Courtrai, in Belgium, and selected his JG staff. His *Jasta* 11 technical officer, the capable Ltn d R Constantin Krefft, assumed the same position for the entire *Geschwader*. For the crucial job of JG I adjutant Richthofen succeeded in having Oblt Karl Bodenschatz transferred from *Jasta* Boelcke. In 1935 Bodenschatz would write the history of *Jagdgeschwader* I, entitled *Jagd in Flanderns Himmel*.

The four component *Staffeln* converged on an area called Marckebeeke, in the vicinity of Marcke, southwest of Courtrai. Staff officers and *Jasta* 11 officers were billeted in Marcke in the castle and estate of Baron Jean de

Vfw Aloys Heldmann appears properly nonchalant after his '*Damenlandung*' (ladies' landing) in Albatros D II D.490/16 in his early days at *Jasta* 10. Heldmann was one of the first members of this *Staffel*, and he gave sterling service in the unit through to the end of war, twice filling the role of acting commander. He ended the war with 15 confirmed victories, and lived to be one of the last survivors of the *Geschwader*

Béthune – comfortable accommodations indeed. *Jastas* 4 and 11 shared the airfield at Marcke, and *Jasta* 10 would soon move to Marckebeeke from nearby Heule. *Jasta* 6 was based at Bisseghem, across the River Lys. Richthofen would continue to live, dine and fly with his old *Jasta* 11. By 2 July all was ready, as Karl Bodenschatz wrote;

'Once the *Staffeln* were assembled at the airfield, 12 machines stood behind each *Staffel* leader. The assembled *Geschwader* appears extremely colourful'.

Richthofen called his *Jasta* leaders together and apprised them of the tactical situation in the area – the enemy's breakthrough efforts in Flanders were being intensified, and German troops were suffering terribly under massive artillery barrages directed by reconnaissance aircraft. The infantry was also being strafed and bombed by low-flying fighters, and 'whole clusters' of bombers attacked the rear areas. The Rittmeister's directions were terse and direct – their assignment was 'destruction of the infantry-support aircraft, destruction of the single-seater fighters, destruction of the bombers'.

Richthofen wanted *Geschwader* operations to be guided by enemy aerial activity in the area. He had direct communications established with observation posts at the frontlines, and had (Bodenschatz wrote);

'A circular telephone link to his four *Staffeln* so that, when he lifts the receiver, all four answer simultaneously. He puts his four *Staffeln* into action only when necessary, but then at a hellish pace. The machines are lined up, the pilots fully dressed next to them, the mechanics ready to swing the propellers at any second. If the take-off order comes, the *Staffel* can roar off inside of a minute.'

Rarely was the entire *Geschwader* deployed in one formation, but Richthofen had plans for eventual deployment of two or three *Staffeln* together. The sequence of daily morning take-offs, in rotation, was *Staffeln* 11, 10, 6 and 4, while the daily midday (1330 to 1500 hrs) take-off sequence was *Staffeln* 10, 6, 4 and 11.

Despite all of his responsibilities, Richthofen still found the time to fly. Fittingly, he would score the first victory for JG I on the morning of 2 July, when he led a patrol of *Jasta* 11 Albatros D Vs against a pair of RE 8s. The witness statements duly gathered for his 57th victory recorded;

'In the direction of Hollebeke, an RE shot down in flames by a red Albatros. Two occupants jumped out.'

The other RE 8 fell to the accurate fire of Ltn Gisbert-Wilhelm Groos for his third confirmed claim. The next day (3 July) brought an unsettling tragedy. *Jasta* 10's CO, Ltn Dossenbach, got into a fight with four British aircraft, but this time, however, it was the attacking Albatros that burst into flame and Dossenbach who jumped to his death. He was hurriedly replaced by Oblt Ernst Freiherr von Althaus from *Jasta* 14. Von Althaus also wore the *Pour le Mérite,* and had flown Eindeckers during the glory days of the 'Fokker Scourge', racking up eight victories. However, he had not scored for

Another photograph taken at Gontrode, this shot shows a Gotha G IV in the huge zeppelin hangar, and offers a better view of the two *Jasta* 11 D Vs. It is believed the fighter at left was one of Richthofen's, as it appears to be entirely overpainted (including the wings) with a thin coat of red. The serial number cannot be discerned, but it is known that the Rittmeister flew D V D.1177/17 for his 54th through 56th victories in late June, and this aircraft was described as having a 'red body' in his combat reports. The D V seen at left may well have been D.1177/17

almost a year. Even a man of von Althaus' accomplishments would have to prove himself to Richthofen, and his uncertain tenure at *Jasta* 10 would depend on his performance.

On 6 July, at 1030 hrs, Richthofen led a group of *Jasta* 11 fighters on a sortie to the southwest. They spotted a flight of FE 2d 'pushers' from No 20 Sqn and circled around to the west of them. *Jasta* 11 attacked the two-seaters at a height of 3000 metres.

As Richthofen closed in on the rearmost FE, he saw it turn to engage him, and was amused to see the observer/gunner open fire at him at a range of over 300 metres. The Rittmeister had not yet even cleared his guns, for, as he wrote, 'One does not score at that distance. Suddenly, I received a blow to my head! I was hit!' Richthofen had received a hammer blow behind his left ear, and was immediately paralysed. The hit had also affected his optic nerve, blinding him. He kept his nerve, and slowly managed to regain some movement, shutting off the engine.

Almost through sheer force of will, his vision slowly returned, and he saw his altimeter registered 800 metres. He restarted the engine and looked overhead to see the Albatros fighters of Ltns Niederhoff and Brauneck, who had followed him down, shepherding their wounded commander. Somehow, he made a remarkably good landing, and the two *Jasta* 11 pilots landed nearby to assist him. Richthofen was rushed to Field Hospital 76 in Courtrai, where it was found he had a ten-centimetre wide patch of bone laid bare, and a severe concussion. He would be out of action for some time. Oblt von Döring assumed acting command of JG I.

It has long been generally believed that Richthofen was brought down by fire from the Lewis gun of observer 2Lt A E Woodbridge of No 20 Sqn, in the FE 2d piloted by Capt D C Cunnell. However, it seems unlikely that the valiant gunner could have hit him from a range of 300 metres, especially to produce a wound on the *back* of Richthofen's skull. In fact, the late historian A E Ferko postulated that Richthofen may have been hit accidentally by fire from one of his own pilots. This theory adds another controversy to the many surrounding Richthofen.

Whatever the cause, JG I was without its revered leader as it went into battle in the furious summer days in Flanders.

The ringmaster falls. On 6 July 1917, the newly-appointed *Geschwader* commander von Richthofen was lucky to survive a glancing head wound during an attack on FE 2B aircraft of No 20 Sqn. Temporarily blinded, he regained his sight just in time to make this remarkably good landing. Although the serial number of this D V is unknown, it was probably the same aircraft the Rittmeister flew for his 57th victory of four days earlier. The scout was described as having a red cowling, tail and wings. Judging from this photograph, even the crosses on the wings were thinly overpainted red. The fuselage cross presents a subdued appearance, possibly caused by an extra coat of varnish that was applied over the national insignia

FLANDERS SUMMER

On the day following Richthofen's fall – 7 July – the dawn brought a perfect arena for combat in the form of a nearly cloudless sky. The night before, Bodenschatz recalled, the pilots of the *Geschwader* displayed 'a certain pensive tension, and in their eyes was a certain concentrated hardness'.

As soon as British artillery spotters were reported in the Ypres salient, aircraft of *Jastas* 4, 6 and 11 took off under von Döring's leadership. The gaggle of JG I fighters came across three Albatros from *Jasta* 24 struggling with two Sopwith 1½ Strutters from No 45 Sqn and their escort of six Sopwith Triplanes from 1 Naval Squadron RNAS. The *Geschwader* pilots waded in, and in short order Niederhoff and Wolff of *Jasta* 11 despatched two of the Triplanes (Wolff's 33rd victory) and *Jasta* 4's Ltn d R Krüger claimed another. Although Altemeier of *Jasta* 24 also claimed a 'Tripehound', three in fact were lost – still, a devastating day for 'Naval 1'.

Around noon, pilots of *Jasta* 6 attacked British two-seaters, resulting in successful claims for aces Krebs (his sixth) and Dostler (14th). Further combats in the afternoon and evening led to three kills for *Jasta* 4 (including Klein's 14th) and the first success for a joyous Ltn Lautenschlager of *Jasta* 11. In all the *Geschwader* claimed nine aircraft that day, with an injury to Döring during a forced landing as their only casualty.

As was often the case, there were several conflicting claims that needed sorting out after such a successful day (Richard Wenzl of *Jasta* 11 would later call this situation 'the well-known victory squabble'), as the ambitious young pilots disputed who should receive credit for a particular aircraft.

In the German Air Service there were no shared kills, and conflicting claims were often settled by a *'Schiedsgericht'*, or arbitration committee – in this case made up of Ltn Krefft for the *Geschwader* and Oblts von Althaus and Dostler for the *Jastas*. The committee reviewed the various

Albatros D V fighters of *Jasta* 4 display their vivid unit and personal markings in this view, which was probably taken during the summer of 1917. Each pilot's aircraft was identified by a bright colour, or pattern of colours, on the tail, which was usually repeated on the spinner. Even the white polka dot décor of the second D V from the left was carried on the spinner as well. The third aircraft bore vertical stripes in two colours on the tail section (*P Kilduff*)

combat reports and used careful judgment and diplomacy to allow or disallow the claims. Only then could the claims be forwarded to 4. *Armee* Headquarters.

Rainy weather prevented flying until the morning of 11 July, when Kurt Wolff led a *Jasta* 11 patrol east of Ypres. However, one of the Albatros fighters soon returned out of the grey mist and made a hurried landing. *Staffelführer* Wolff climbed carefully from the cockpit, holding his bleeding left hand aloft. The patrol had been jumped by British fighters. With typical dry humour, Wolff wrote to his betrothed;

'Early yesterday, you see, I had my hand out right where an Englishman was shooting. And since my hand made just as little effort to run aside as the bullet did, the bullet, being the harder component, went through the hand – the wrist bone was shot clean through.'

He soon lay in a hospital bed at St Nicholas Hospital, next to Richthofen. That same day, the *Jasta* 4 teenager Wüsthoff flamed a balloon for his 3rd confirmed claim, and his *Staffel* mate Hans Klein got two more 'gasbags' to bring his tally to 16. Mohnicke of *Jasta* 11 and Vfw Patermann of *Jasta* 4 also claimed aircraft, but Patermann's elation over his second victory was short-lived, as he died the next day as the first fatality of JG I.

Following Wolff's wounding, command of *Jasta* 11 was given to Oblt Wilhelm Reinhard, a Regular Army officer from Dusseldorf who had been commissioned in the *Badisches-Fussartillerie Regt* Nr 14 in 1910. He had arrived at *Jasta* 11 in May, and though he had as yet achieved no victories, he had the proper Prussian officer's training and leadership experience – Reinhard would prove more than equal to the task.

'These are breathless days', wrote Bodenschatz, 'One after another, the take-offs. One after another, the victories'. On 12 July, in exchange for the loss of Patermann, *Jasta* 4 airmen claimed two aircraft and *Jasta* 6 added five more (three of them apparently SE 5s from No 56 Sqn). The next day, Friday the 13th, brought both good and bad fortune, with *Jastas* 4 and 6 attacking a group of six Sopwith 1¹/₂ Strutters (of No 70 Sqn) escorted by

An ill-fated quartet of NCO comrades from JG I pose in the initial days of the *Geschwader,* with *Jasta* 4 Albatros D Vs in the background. They are, from left to right, Vfws Fritz Krebs of *Jasta* 6 (eight victories), Linus Patermann of *Jasta* 4 (two victories), Carl Holler of *Jasta* 6 (three victories) and Ernst Clausnitzer of *Jasta* 4. Patermann fell on 12 July 1917 as the first fatal casualty of *Jagdgeschwader* I, and a mere four days later Krebs was killed and Clausnitzer was taken prisoner. Holler survived the war to write his memoirs under his stage name of Niels Sörensen

Nieuports from No 29 Sqn. *Jasta* 4 star Hans Klein was wounded in the attack, but made a successful landing behind German lines. *Jasta* 6 then ravaged the enemy formation, bringing down four of them – Dostler had scored 'doubles' for two days straight to raise his tally to 18, while his friend Hans Adam got his fifth and Fritz Krebs claimed two.

16 July proved another hard day. Vfw Ernst Clausnitzer of *Jasta* 4 attempted an attack on a balloon, but was intercepted by three SPADs of No 23 Sqn and brought down and taken prisoner. The hapless Clausnitzer would experience extremes of treatment from his captors, as he later wrote;

'I immediately attacked the leader's machine but, after the first rounds, both my machine guns jammed. I didn't succeed in clearing the jams because both bolts were stuck fast. In spite of all attempts to escape, I was gradually forced ever lower and, at a height of 50 metres, took a hit in the motor. The motor stopped and I went down in a glide into the fields. I was

Jasta 11 mechanics pose with an Albatros D V said to have been flown by Oblt Reinhard, perhaps in the summer of 1917. The nose back to the cockpit, struts and wheel covers displays the *staffel's* red, while the colour of the personal fuselage band marking remains unknown. Hans Georg von der Osten recalled, 'All of our machines, in any case those of *Jasta* 11, had red-coloured markings on the front of the aeroplane. The individual markings were unique, each pilot having a special one. Sometimes it happened that your own aeroplane was *kaputt* and you took another aircraft with another insignia on it' (*HAC/UTD*)

Ernst Clausnitzer of *Jasta* 4 was flying this Albatros D V (D.1162/17) when he attacked a balloon southeast of Poperinghe in the search for his fourth victory on 16 July. The tables were turned, however, as he was shot down by SPADs of No 23 Sqn RFC, but his D V came down quite intact and, of course, became the subject of close scrutiny. It bore the usual *Jasta* 4 unit marking wrapped about its fuselage, and had a yellow tail and spinner

welcomed by some London artillerymen with a sound thrashing, removed by some officers, and in the evening I was handed over to the airmen, with whom I spent four days as their guest.'

On the same day, No 56 Sqn again tangled with JG I, and the rising career of *Jasta* 6 pilot Fritz Krebs (eight victories) came to an end when he was shot down by Capt G Bowman in a swirling melee northeast of Zonnebeke – he was Bowman's 10th of 32 victories. These losses were offset to some extent by Adam's sixth victory and Kurt Wüsthoff's fourth claim (a balloon).

Hard times persisted as the 'murderous tempo' of aerial combat over the Ypres Salient continued. On 17 July Ltn d R Richard Krüger of *Jasta* 4 was severely wounded at midday, and he died several hours later. That same evening, JG I took on Camels of No 70 Sqn and two Sopwiths were downed, with credits going to Ltn Robert Tüxen (*Jasta* 6) for his first and the fast-rising Wüsthoff for his fifth. However, *Jasta* 11 pilot Ltn d R Karl 'Carlos' Meyer was wounded by ace Capt Noel Webb. He was the latter's seventh claim.

Karl Meyer was born in Caracas of a German father and Venezuelan mother, and was known as Carlos Meyer Baldo in his native land (he had returned to Germany in 1908, and had served in the 8th Cuirassier Regiment before entering aviation). His wound was not serious, and he would soon be back in action.

These continuing losses spurred acting *Geschwader* commander von Döring to alter the unit's tactics, as specified in this order;

'After the experiences of the last few days, it has been shown that the *Staffeln* flying individually are not in the position to successfully combat the strong English squadrons appearing mainly in the evenings. Simultaneous deployment of the *Geshwader Staffeln* is therefore necessary, and will be ensured from now on by existing order of the *Geschwader*.

A relieved Robert Tüxen (second from left) of *Jasta* 6 poses with his groundcrew to commemorate a narrow escape. It would appear that the synchronisation gear on his Albatros D V malfunctioned, and the machine guns severed one propeller blade. The resulting vibration nearly shook the engine from its mountings, as evident here. Also visible are the black and white stripe unit markings of *Jasta* 6 on the elevator and underside of the bottom wing

The *Staffeln* must appear at the Front at the same time, at high altitude (4000-5000 metres) and carry out the attack on strong English squadrons as close to the same time as possible. For the time being, the deployment of the entire *Geschwader* shall be limited to the evening hours. During combat patrols of the individual *Staffeln* during the course of the day, attacking mainly those artillery-spotting and reconnaissance aircraft flying at low altitude is recommended.

Richthofen, recuperating in his hospital room at Courtrai, must have boiled with anger as he read von Döring's report. For some time Richthofen had been at odds with his immediate superior, *Kofl* of the 4. *Armee,* Hptm Otto Bufe. Richthofen blamed Bufe for instituting a required timetable whereby the individual *Staffeln* were ordered on fruitless 'barrier flights' (*Sperrflüge*), instead of massing the aircraft of the *Geschwader* on more purposeful fighter sorties.

Richthofen sent off an intemperate letter to his high-placed friend Oblt Fritz von Falkenhayn, criticising Bufe's misuse of the *Geschwader.* It was to prove unnecessary, as on the same day (19 July) the commander of the entire 4. *Armee,* Gen Sixt von Arnim, gave an order for increased attacks against the bothersome British captive balloons, freeing up the JG I pilots. '*Jagdgeschwader* I is equally available to sweep the attack zone free of enemy aircraft.' The new tactics paid off handsomely, for on the 21st and 22nd, *Jagdstaffeln* 4, 6 and 11 achieved 13 kills with no losses. These successes were achieved with what were, according to Richthofen, obsolete Albatros D IIIs and D Vs. In the same letter cited above, he wrote;

'Our aircraft are laughingly inferior to the English. Their Triplane and 200-hp SPAD, as well as the Sopwith single-seater, play with our D V. But the people at home have not brought out anything new for almost a year, except this lousy Albatros, and have remained stuck with the D III design which I flew combat missions with in the autumn of last year. Not only do the English single-seaters climb better and are faster than we are, the British have also developed a two-seater (the Bristol F 2B) that our Albatros cannot match – it can easily outclimb the Albatros in a curve.'

When he paid a brief visit to Marckebeeke on 20 July, Richthofen had tried to raise the spirits of his men by telling them, 'You will receive new Fokker triplanes, which climb like apes and are as manoeuvrable as the devil'. The new Fokkers, however, would be regrettably long in coming.

There was some good news for Richthofen, though. Whether due to his influence or not, Hptm Bufe was reassigned as *Kofl* of the 8. *Armee* on the Eastern Front on 5 August. He was succeeded by Hptm Hellmuth Wilberg, who would maintain a close relationship with Richthofen.

THE RETURN OF THE RITTMEISTER

Manfred von Richthofen had returned to Marckebeeke on 25 July, and was soon back in the saddle as *Geschwader* commander. This was in spite of his prominently bandaged head wound, still unhealed, which would continue to plague him with headaches – he was not yet permitted to fly. He must have been pleased with the recent successes of his unit, but saddened on 26 July when he lost yet another one of his young protégés from *Jasta* 11.

In a huge dogfight involving RFC Camels, Pups, SE 5s and SPADs, Ltn d R Otto Brauneck (a 21-year-old with ten victories) was shot down

After his return to the *Geschwader*, Richthofen sat on the steps of Chateau Marckebeeke on 30 July as his old friend Erwin Böhme paid a visit. From left to right on the front step are JG I technical officer Constantin Krefft, Richthofen, Eberhardt Mohnicke and Böhme. At the extreme left in the second row is possibly Oblt Reinhard, then Ltn von Schönebeck, Oblt Guido Scheffer (*Jasta* 11 OzbV) and Ltn d R Wilhelm Bockelmann, but the rest cannot be identified with certainty

and killed south of Zonnebeke. His Albatros may have been claimed by Capt Noel Webb of No 70 Sqn, who had shot down Meyer on the 17th.

28 July brought a spectacular bag of 12 confirmed victories to JG I, eight of them being credited to the leading unit of the *Geschwader* at this time, *Jasta* 6. The successes on this date would result in high honours for the participants.

The day began with kills by Vfw Küllmer and Hans Adam of *Jasta* 6, as well as the second victory of Ltn Bockelmann of *Jasta* 11.

At around 1850 hrs that evening, a flight of six DH 4 bombers of No 57 Sqn were returning from a raid on Ingelmunster. *Jasta* 6 commander Oblt Eduard Dostler (along with his deputy leader Adam) led his pilots in a well-coordinated interception sortie. As the Germans closed in on the bomber formation, Adam's aircraft was hit in a potentially dangerous location. Nonetheless, he suddenly dived into the tight formation of

This No 70 Sqn Camel B3823 (coded 'C 5') was forced down behind German lines as part of the carnage inflicted by JG I on 28 July 1917. The pilot, 2Lt R C Hume, survived as a PoW. The Camel is generally credited as the victim of Ltn Eberhardt Mohnicke of *Jasta* 11, who claimed a 'BE 1-seater' at 2100 hrs at Becelaere-Moorslede for his fourth victory. No 70 Sqn lost another Camel at the same time, Oblt von Boenigk of *Jasta* 4 and Oblt Weigand of *Jasta* 10 also making successful claims for Sopwith '1-seaters' (*HAC/UTD*)

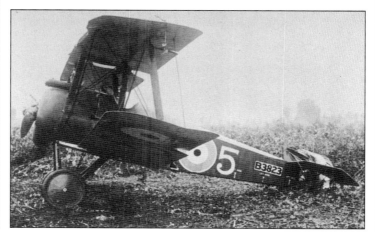

DH 4s, forcing the big two-seaters to break and scatter. This allowed the other *Jasta* 6 pilots to pick off the disorganised bombers, and they proceeded to devastate the formation. Dostler received credit for two, Adam claimed another for his tenth and Ltns Tüxen, Czermak and Stock each claimed one as well. The jubilant *Jasta* 6 pilots landed back at Bisseghem airfield to report that they had destroyed the entire flight of six bombers, all within the German lines.

The *Kofl* 4 report on this fight confirmed all six victories, and Hans Adam would earn the prestigious Knight's Cross of the Military Max-Joseph Order for his part in the action, making him Ritter von Adam. Furthermore, with his score now at 20, Dostler would certainly be awarded the *Pour le Mérite* before long.

However, only three DH 4s of No 57 Squadron were actually brought down, the remaining three having limped home badly shot up. The wreckage of three bombers was located by *Kofl* 4 staff, but no more. According to historian A E Ferko, this embarrassing situation led *Kofl* 4 to realise that the confirmations had been issued prematurely, but they were not revoked. On 11 October *Kofl* 4 released new guidelines for the confirmation of victories. 'In the future, claims will only be accepted when supported by eyewitness reports from the ground or the air'.

Nonetheless, *Jasta* 6 had achieved 28 confirmed victories in July, making it the group's leading *Staffel*. *Jasta* 10, on the other hand, had recorded a comparatively poor performance – just seven victories in June and July. Richthofen's critical eye fell on the *Staffelführer*, the highly-decorated, but seemingly ineffective, Oblt Ernst Freiherr von Althaus. The *Jasta* 10 leader had succeeded in downing a Camel on 24 July for his

Ltn d L Hans Ritter von Adam of *Jasta* 6 was 31-years-old when he took part in the *Jasta* 6 victories on 28 July 1917, and later led the *Jasta*. Hans Schröder described him as, 'a real father to his *Staffel*. He was considerably older than his pilots, and had a wife and children at home. Adam was not a greedy fighter who wanted all the victories for himself. He always left the "simple cases" to his companions, and saw that they had plenty of opportunities to use their guns and backed their claims'

Reportedly excited over his second victory (part of the attack on DH 4s of No 57 Sqn on 28 July), Ltn d R Robert Tüxen hams it up for the camera. His Albatros D V bore a thinly-painted white fuselage band with narrow black borders, just visible here. This D V also bore the *Staffel* markings of broad black and white stripes on its tailplane and beneath the lower wing

A longtime *Jasta* 10 mechanic, Xaver Leinmüller sits in the Albatros D III flown by Vfw Ernst Günther Burggaller. Like most other *Jasta* 10 aircraft of the summer of 1917, this D III displayed the unit marking of a chrome yellow nose and struts, and was identified by a small number ('7' in this case) painted on the forward fuselage. The pilot's personal marking was a white bar that extended back to the fuselage cross. The wheels were additionally marked, probably in black and white or yellow and white. This D III had been substantially modified at the *Jasta*, with small auxiliary struts at the base of the interplane struts, and an unusual headrest fitted behind the cockpit (both features usually associated with the D V). Burggaller scored no victories during his seven months in *Jasta* 10, but he became a well-known motorcycle and auto racer in the interwar years. He served in the Luftwaffe in World War 2 and was killed in action in early 1940

ninth victory, but it was his first success in a year. A week later Richthofen sacked von Althaus from his command.

Over the years various reasons have been put forth, including Althaus' failing eyesight (he would, indeed, later go blind). Recently, more information has come to light. Historian H J Nowarra described von Althaus diplomatically. 'He liked the games and the girls, and he took life as a game – he enjoyed poker.' In a more blunt vein, Hptm Erich Serno, the leader of the Turkish Army Air Service, had refused the transfer of von Althaus to his command because, 'Von Althaus was famous among aviators for gambling, his love of women and even worse habits'.

It would seem that the dashing hussar and *bon vivant* had a serious gambling problem, and incurred major debts even at *Jasta* 10. This, combined with his mediocre leadership, resulted in him being posted to a *Jasta* school as an instructor.

On 30 July von Althaus' replacement arrived at *Jasta* 10. Twenty-year-old Ltn Werner Voss was one of Richthofen's old friends from *Jasta* Boelcke, and he was described as being 'very young and wiry, with 34 victories behind him'. Voss was at this time Richthofen's closest rival in terms of victories, and a charismatic and daring figure. Time would tell if he could handle the heavy responsibilities of command.

A little known *Jasta* 10 pilot named Vfw Bansmer flew this Albatros D V. The mechanic on the left (as always) obscures much of the serial number, but it was most likely D.1187/17. This was another early production D V with a headrest. Aside from the usual chrome yellow nose, this Albatros displayed the pilot's personal markings of a black and white quartering, or 'chequerboard', on the fuselage and beneath each lower wing. This motif was repeated on the wheel covers as well. Note the rack of flare cartridges and the flare pistol mounted on the side of the cockpit, along with the rear view mirror

THE THIRD BATTLE OF YPRES BEGINS

The tremendous tension that had been building all along the Flanders Front broke at 0350 hrs on 31 July with a gigantic French and British attack – the Third Battle of Ypres. Despite uninterrupted rain and low ceiling, waves of RFC and RNAS aircraft flew far behind the German lines and gained *de facto* aerial supremacy. JG I aircraft did not even fly until 1100 hrs, in response to an attack on *Armee Gruppe* Wytschaete. Nonetheless, the *Geschwader* brought down five aircraft that cloudy day, including one each for Dostler and Wüsthoff.

Heavy rains followed on the first three days of August. On the 4th and 5th three aircraft fell to the guns of *Jasta* 4, as Wüsthoff claimed his eighth and promising Silesian Ltn Oskar Freiherr von Boenigk brought down a Sopwith for his third.

The night of 6 August was a festive one in the officers' *Kasino* of *Jasta* 6, as the airmen gathered to celebrate the award of the *Pour le Mérite* to their commander, Oblt Eduard Dostler, whose bag stood at 21. Richthofen himself dropped in on the party. Since Dostler's medal would be some days in arriving, the Rittmeister generously removed his own 'Blue Max' and hung it around Dostler's neck for the inevitable photograph. The following day Kurt Wolff returned to JG I, although like Richthofen, he was still forbidden to fly.

On 10 August the mercurial Werner Voss made his first entry in the *Geschwader* 'game book' when he led *Jasta* 10 in an attack on some French SPAD XIIIs of SPA31. Despite their inferior Albatros machines, Voss and Uffz Herman Brettel each downed one of the new SPADs near Klerken. Ltn Stock of *Jasta* 6 added a Sopwith for a *Geschwader* total of three for the day, in exchange for the loss of Ltn d R Oskar Rouselle of *Jasta* 4 – he was wounded, but would return to the unit some months later.

On 11 August 1917, 21-year-old Ltn Hans-Georg von der Osten joined *Jasta* 11, having already seen service with F. Fl. Abt. 69, and having undergone a very brief instruction at *Jastaschule* I. In the early 1970s von

This OAW-built Albatros D III was flown by Vfw Kurt Wüsthoff, and the *Jasta* 4 spiral marking is evident. It is believed that the tail section was painted black(?), with white elevators and rudder, and the spinner was divided into half black, half white segments as well

WERNER VOSS

Werner Voss was born in Krefeld on 13 April 1887. When he was 27, he enlisted in his local militia, then went to war with the 2. *Westfälische Husaren-Regiment* Nr 11 – a unit known as the 'dancing hussars'. Like so many other cavalrymen, the stalemate of trench warfare failed to meet his expectations, and he transferred into aviation in August 1915. Once trained, Voss was assigned to *Kasta* 20 of *Kagohl* IV, and he began his career as a military pilot in the Verdun area. He was happily transferred to *Jasta* Boelcke on 21 November, and started out his victory string with a double only six days later. It was here that he first met Richthofen.

Voss scored rapidly in February and March, and on the 17th of the latter month he received the Knight's Cross with Swords of the Royal Hohenzollern House Order (the 'Hohenzollern'). With his tally at 24, he received the 'Blue Max' on 8 April. This was followed by routine leave, during which Voss missed most of the killing time of 'Bloody April'. In May 1917 he returned to *Jasta* Boelcke and brought his score to 28 (12 of them being hapless BE 2s), but the young fighter ace – he had just turned 20 – was dissatisfied with his *Staffelführer*, the veteran Hptm Franz Walz. Along with another misguided young pilot (Ltn von Lersner), Werner Voss submitted charges to *Kofl* 2 that

Walz was 'war-weary', and that an elite unit like *Jasta* Boelcke required a more dynamic leader. Their blatant disregard for the military code of conduct and the chain of command saw both pilots posted out of the prestigious *Jasta*. Voss received a severe reprimand, but his youth and record kept him from harsher punishment.

Voss was given acting command of *Jasta* 5 on 20 May, then a scant nine days later went to *Jasta* 29. His time as *Staffelführer* only lasted five days, whereupon he went to command *Jasta* 14. He seems to have cared little for the responsibilities of command, and despised paperwork.

At the end of July 1917 Voss' old comrade Richthofen called upon him to replace von Althaus as leader of *Jasta* 10, and Voss was soon building up the score of that lacklustre unit. He briefly flew a Pfalz D III and an Albatros D V with *Jagdstaffel* 10. On 18 October (a few weeks after Voss' death) a British airman named B B Perry was shot down by Löwenhardt and taken prisoner. Perry was given a tour of *Jasta* 10's airfield, the *Jasta* pilots pointing out a 'bright green' Albatros they said had been Voss'. At any rate, Voss is rightly associated with Fokker F I 103/17 – the machine in which he scored the last of his 48 kills, and in which he met his death in the storied clash with No 56 Sqn on 23 September 1917.

The mercurial and aggressive commander of *Jasta* 10, Werner Voss

der Osten was interviewed by L Zacharias and M Thiemeyer, and his narrative provides a glimpse of what a new JG I pilot experienced;

'Oblt Reinhard had taken command of the *Staffel*, and I had to make a short demonstration flight for him. I took the opportunity to fly over Courtrai. When I landed, Reinhard was still standing there and said, "Yes, you'll do".

'Immediately thereafter, I flew on patrol against some Englishmen who had been reported. Everything was so new to me on this sortie, especially flying in close formation. Then suddenly I saw some cockades –

Englishmen! I managed to get rid of some of my bullets, but I stuck close to Reinhard so that I did not get lost. If you are not familiar with a new area, this is always a bit hard. Then, however, I learned quickly, and by the third day was having tougher air fights on my own.'

14 August began badly when *Jasta* 11's youthful Ltn Hans Joachim Wolff (known as '*Wolffchen*', or 'Little Wolff', to distinguish him from Kurt Wolff) was wounded in the thigh over Zillebeke Lake at 0920 hrs. Like his namesake, he wound up in St Nicholas Hospital in Courtrai. *Jasta* 10 was finally scoring again, however, as Löwenhardt and Oblt Weigand each tallied their second victories.

As Richthofen expected of his *Staffel* leaders, Reinhard of *Staffel* 11 led by example, bringing down his second and third enemy aircraft, and his pilots Ltn d R Franz Müller and 'Carlos' Meyer – now back in action – each brought down Sopwiths. The deadly *Jasta* 6 team of Dostler and Adam also scored over Sopwiths in the evening, but the group's elation was dampened when the promising Saxon Ltn Alfred Hübener (four victories) of *Staffel* 4 was shot down near Moorslede at 2035 hrs. He probably fell to the Nieuport ace Capt Tom Falcon Hazell MC of No 1 Sqn as the 18th of an eventual 43 victories. It was not the last time that Hazell would meet *Jasta* 4 in combat.

Pilots of JG I were occasionally assigned to provide escort duty for the bombers of KG 1, as on the 15th when they met up with the big Friedrichshafens over Orchies, but their operations were hampered by bad weather. The following day *Kofl* 4 again ordered JG I to provide one *Staffel* for a bombing raid on Poperinghe and another for a two-seater attack on the machine-gun nests near Zillebeke Lake.

More important for the pilots and crews of JG I, however, was the fact that their revered Rittmeister had returned to the air on the 16th. Only 40 days after suffering his head wound, Richthofen took off in his red Albatros D V D.2059/17 and led a morning sortie of *Jasta* 11, his head still heavily bandaged. Determined to show he had lost neither his skill nor his nerve, he attacked four Nieuports of No 29 Sqn;

Ltn Hans Joachim Wolff had been commissioned in the *Schleswig-Holsteinisches Ulanen-Regiment* Nr 15 before serving as a pilot in Fl. Abt. (A) 216. The 'yellow Uhlan' joined *Jasta* 11 on 6 July 1917, but had an unlucky start as a fighter pilot. On 14 August 1917 Wolff was wounded in the thigh, possibly by Sopwith Triplanes of 1 Naval Squadron. He returned to *Jasta* 11, only to be slightly injured when he overturned his Albatros upon landing at Avesnes le Sec. A popular member of the *Staffel*, he was known as '*Wölffchen*' or 'Little Wolff', to distinguish him from Kurt Wolff

By the summer of 1917, the red colouration of *Jasta* 11 aircraft had been standardised as a true unit marking. These Albatros D Vs of the Richthofen *Staffel* all display the red noses, struts and wheel covers which were characteristic of the *Jasta*. Richthofen himself specified that the tail surfaces were the best location for personal colours, as exemplified here. The machine second from left belonged to Ltn d R Franz Müller, who scored two victories with *Jasta* 11. Its tail was white, supplemented by a green fuselage band bordered with a white stripe. At the extreme upper right is D V D.2161/17, which was flown by Ltn Hans-Carl von Linsingen and appears to only bear the *Staffel* colours. Note that the first and fourth aircraft from the right had five-colour lozenge fabric on their wings, while the middle two displayed painted camouflage

'After a short fight, I shot up his engine and fuel tank. The aeroplane went into a tail spin. I immediately followed it until just above the ground. The aeroplane crashed southwest of Houthulst Forest and ran into the ground. Since I had followed him down to about 50 metres, I came into a cloud of gas and, for a brief moment, I became ill.'

This flight left the Rittmeister exhausted and nauseated, and upon his return to Marckebeeke he went straight to bed. The *Geschwader* scored three other victories that same day, the most notable being Werner Voss' 37th. The 20-year-old *Jasta* 10 commander brought down a Camel over St Julien at 2100 hrs, which was almost certainly flown by 14-victory ace Noel Webb of 70 Sqn, who was killed. Webb was the probable victor over *Jasta* 11 pilots Meyer and Brauneck in the previous month.

A MILESTONE AND A LOSS

A significant milestone was reached by *Jasta* 11 the next day, as related by Hans-Georg von der Osten;

'On the evening of 17 August we had a *Staffel* sortie under the command of Oblt Reinhard. We flew in a northerly direction and we saw a squadron of British Sopwith two-seaters (actually Bristols) above us, flying eastwards. I had the opportunity to attack one of them from below at a favourable angle, and forced him to go immediately into a spiralling, gliding descent. I pursued him, firing several bursts through the clouds until he landed with a crash.

'During the air fight, I had seen a German Navy fighter join us beneath the clouds, and as I watched him fly close over the crashed Englishman, he dropped a message-bag with his address. He later claimed to have scored the victory, but was contradicted by the statements of the wounded pilot, who stated he had been shot down by the "Red Baron" (i.e., von der Osten's red-nosed Albatros).

'On the evening of the same 17 August, the Rittmeister suddenly ordered a bottle of champagne and announced that this, my first victory, had been the 200th victory of *Jasta* 11. I would like to add that it was very rarely that we did any drinking in *Jasta* 11, as we always had to keep ourselves ready for action. This was not true for all – at *Jasta* 4, for instance, under Oblt von Döring, they sometimes had some very wet evenings.'

The congratulatory telegrams for *Jasta* 11 poured in, and coincidentally the *Geschwader* soon hosted a very exalted guest. On 20 August most of the airmen of the 4. *Armee* assembled for a parade before the supreme warlord Kaiser Wilhelm himself. In the place of honour in the frontline were JG I's *Pour le Mérite* airmen Richthofen and Oblt Dostler of *Jasta* 6.

It would be Dostler's last parade. Two days later, the 25-year-old Bavarian led three other *Jasta* 6 Albatros pilots down on an RE 8 of No 7 Sqn, crewed by Lt Sharples and 2Lt O'Callaghan. The observer O'Callaghan opened fire on his attackers from 100 yards, and although he was only able to fire 55 rounds before a jam silenced his Lewis gun, his aim was true. Dostler's D V burst into flames and exploded.

In the dim chance of finding Dostler somewhere hiding in no-man's land, Richthofen sent out flights to look for him, but to no avail. Dostler was buried where he fell, and posthumously received Bavaria's Knight's Cross of the Military Max-Joseph Order.

Jasta 6 ace Ltn Hans Adam wrote off his Albatros D V D.1148/17 in a crash landing on 2 August 1917. Here, the salvage crew from *Jasta* 6 pose with the sorry remains of the Albatros. Adam emerged from the crash unscathed, and would take command of the *Staffel* 20 days later after the death of Ltn Dostler. The white portion of the aft fuselage that was part of the unit marking is visible here, as is Adam's white-bordered black(?) fuselage band (*HAC/UTD*)

According to Bodenschatz, 'The Rittmeister is hit hard by this loss. It is a little quieter in the officers' mess this evening'. Hans Adam, Dostler's friend and deputy CO, was given command of *Jasta* 6. The 31-year-old Adam became a 'real father to his *Staffel*', and would prove a superb leader. The loss of such an old hand as Dostler reinforced the pilots' gloomy opinions about the inferiority of their machines. Nonetheless, they persevered, and downed three enemy fighters on the 23rd. Two days later, von der Osten bagged his second enemy machine through a bit of luck;

'While on a patrol along the frontlines I lost my formation in a turn and suddenly found myself behind some Sopwith Triplanes. Quickly, I came up behind one of them, and with my first burst it nosed down and crashed vertically into the battlefield between Passchendaele and Langemarck'.

The pilot, 2Lt Lewis of 10 Naval Squadron, became a PoW.

On 26 August the airfields at Heule, Bisseghem and Marcke were strafed by SPADs of No 19 Sqn. In response to this (and in virtual defiance of orders forbidding him to fly), Richthofen took off with four others from *Jasta* 11 and soon found one of the SPADs above solid cloud;

'I attacked him, coming out of the sun. Upon pursuit, I saw him, under the cloud cover, first plunge straight down and then explode in the air at a height of 500 metres. Due to the new, very poor incendiary ammunition, my pressure line, intake manifold, exhaust, etc were so damaged that I couldn't have pursued even a crippled opponent.'

The Rittmeister managed to glide back safely, but this episode must have heightened his disgust with his inferior equipment. On 28 August he wrote, 'I have made only two combat flights, and both were successful, but after each flight I was completely exhausted. My wound is healing frightfully slowly'.

On that same day, however, there was finally good news for Richthofen and the airmen of JG I. The first of the long-awaited, and highly anticipated, Fokker triplanes had arrived. In spite of rainy weather, Werner Voss made the first test-flights of Fokker F I 103/17 that evening. The *Geschwader* pilots viewed the arrival of these distinctive new machines with great expectations.

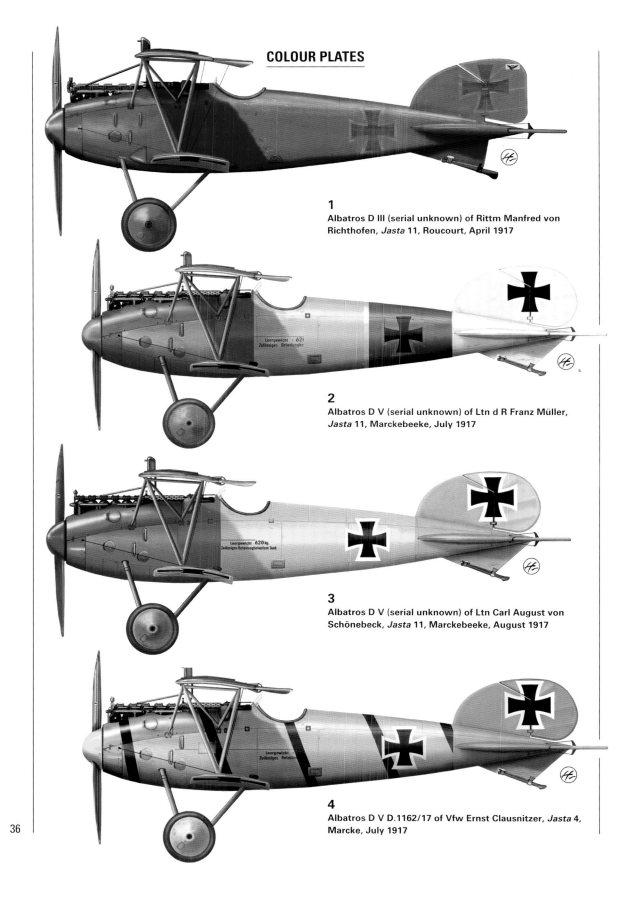

COLOUR PLATES

1
Albatros D III (serial unknown) of Rittm Manfred von Richthofen, *Jasta* 11, Roucourt, April 1917

2
Albatros D V (serial unknown) of Ltn d R Franz Müller, *Jasta* 11, Marckebeeke, July 1917

3
Albatros D V (serial unknown) of Ltn Carl August von Schönebeck, *Jasta* 11, Marckebeeke, August 1917

4
Albatros D V D.1162/17 of Vfw Ernst Clausnitzer, *Jasta* 4, Marcke, July 1917

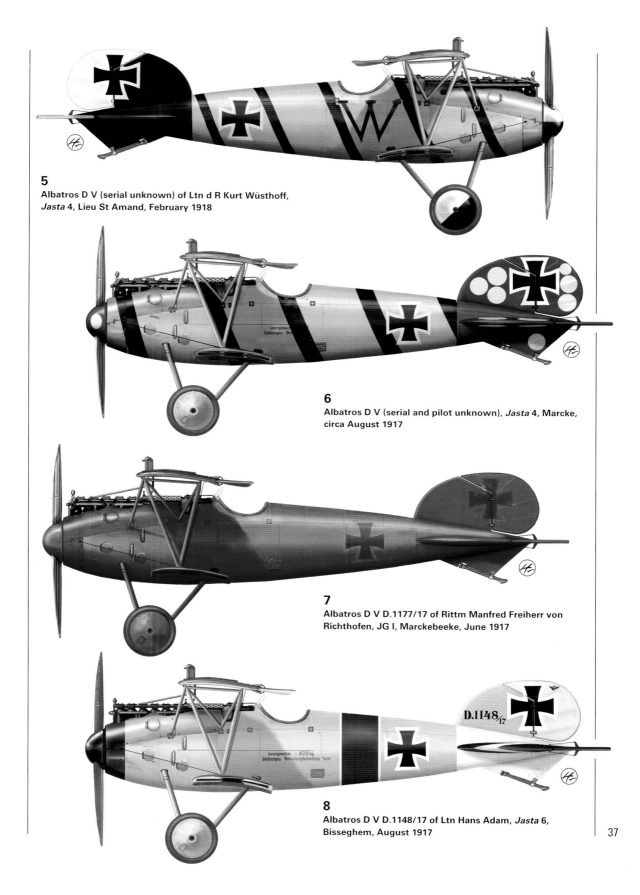

5
Albatros D V (serial unknown) of Ltn d R Kurt Wüsthoff,
Jasta 4, Lieu St Amand, February 1918

6
Albatros D V (serial and pilot unknown), *Jasta* 4, Marcke,
circa August 1917

7
Albatros D V D.1177/17 of Rittm Manfred Freiherr von
Richthofen, JG I, Marckebeeke, June 1917

8
Albatros D V D.1148/17 of Ltn Hans Adam, *Jasta* 6,
Bisseghem, August 1917

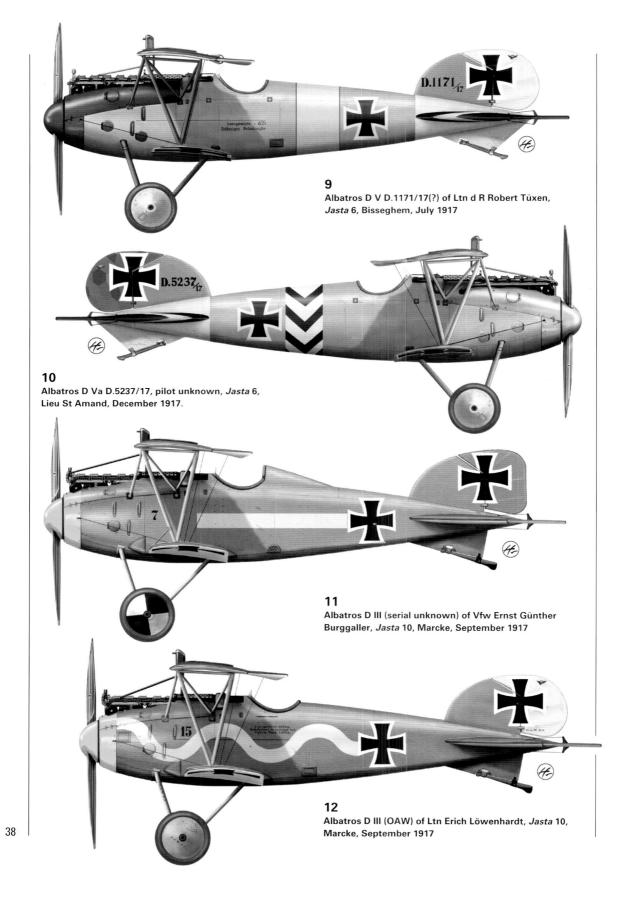

9
Albatros D V D.1171/17(?) of Ltn d R Robert Tüxen,
Jasta 6, Bisseghem, July 1917

10
Albatros D Va D.5237/17, pilot unknown, *Jasta* 6,
Lieu St Amand, December 1917.

11
Albatros D III (serial unknown) of Vfw Ernst Günther
Burggaller, *Jasta* 10, Marcke, September 1917

12
Albatros D III (OAW) of Ltn Erich Löwenhardt, *Jasta* 10,
Marcke, September 1917

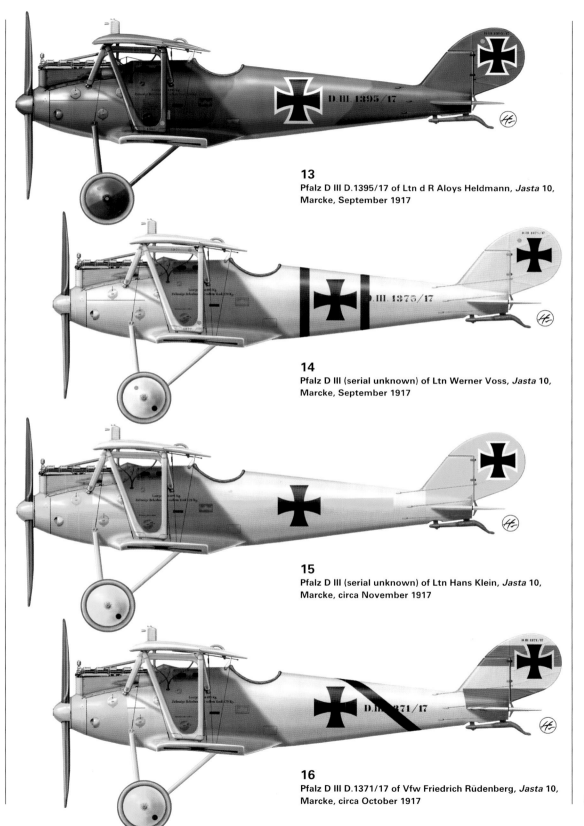

13
Pfalz D III D.1395/17 of Ltn d R Aloys Heldmann, *Jasta* 10,
Marcke, September 1917

14
Pfalz D III (serial unknown) of Ltn Werner Voss, *Jasta* 10,
Marcke, September 1917

15
Pfalz D III (serial unknown) of Ltn Hans Klein, *Jasta* 10,
Marcke, circa November 1917

16
Pfalz D III D.1371/17 of Vfw Friedrich Rüdenberg, *Jasta* 10,
Marcke, circa October 1917

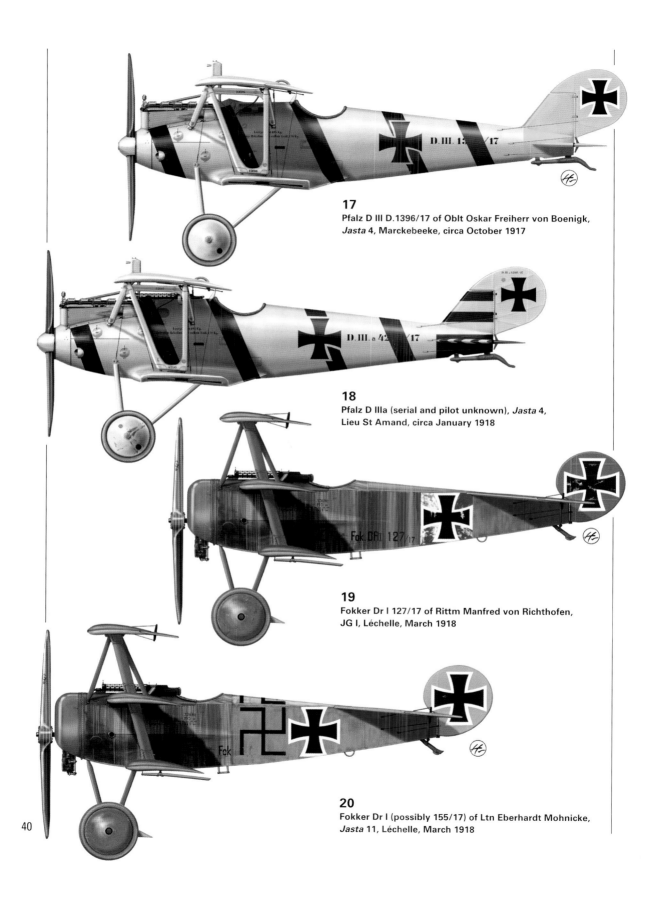

17
Pfalz D III D.1396/17 of Oblt Oskar Freiherr von Boenigk,
Jasta 4, Marckebeeke, circa October 1917

18
Pfalz D IIIa (serial and pilot unknown), *Jasta* 4,
Lieu St Amand, circa January 1918

19
Fokker Dr I 127/17 of Rittm Manfred von Richthofen,
JG I, Léchelle, March 1918

20
Fokker Dr I (possibly 155/17) of Ltn Eberhardt Mohnicke,
Jasta 11, Léchelle, March 1918

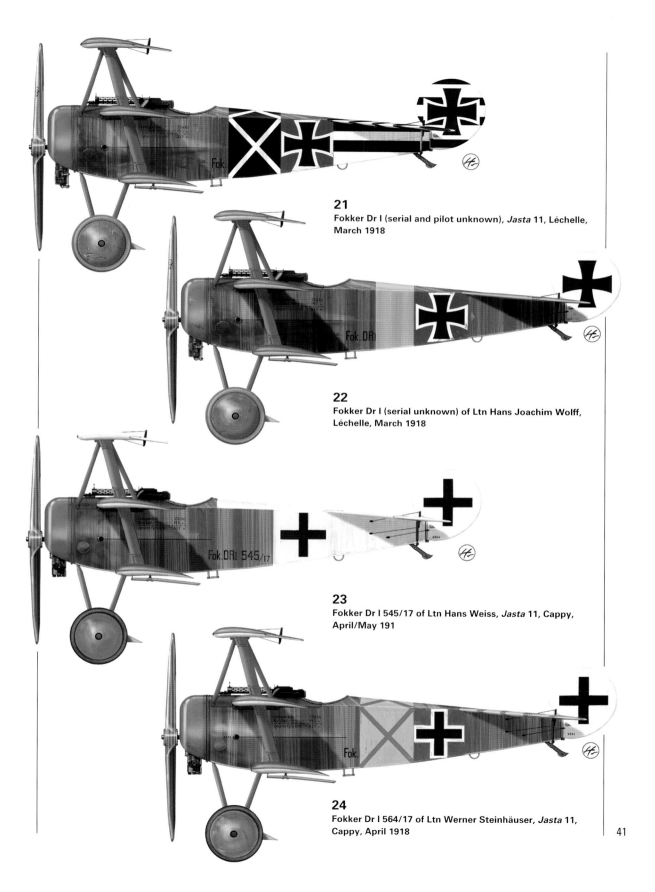

21
Fokker Dr I (serial and pilot unknown), *Jasta* 11, Léchelle,
March 1918

22
Fokker Dr I (serial unknown) of Ltn Hans Joachim Wolff,
Léchelle, March 1918

23
Fokker Dr I 545/17 of Ltn Hans Weiss, *Jasta* 11, Cappy,
April/May 191

24
Fokker Dr I 564/17 of Ltn Werner Steinhäuser, *Jasta* 11,
Cappy, April 1918

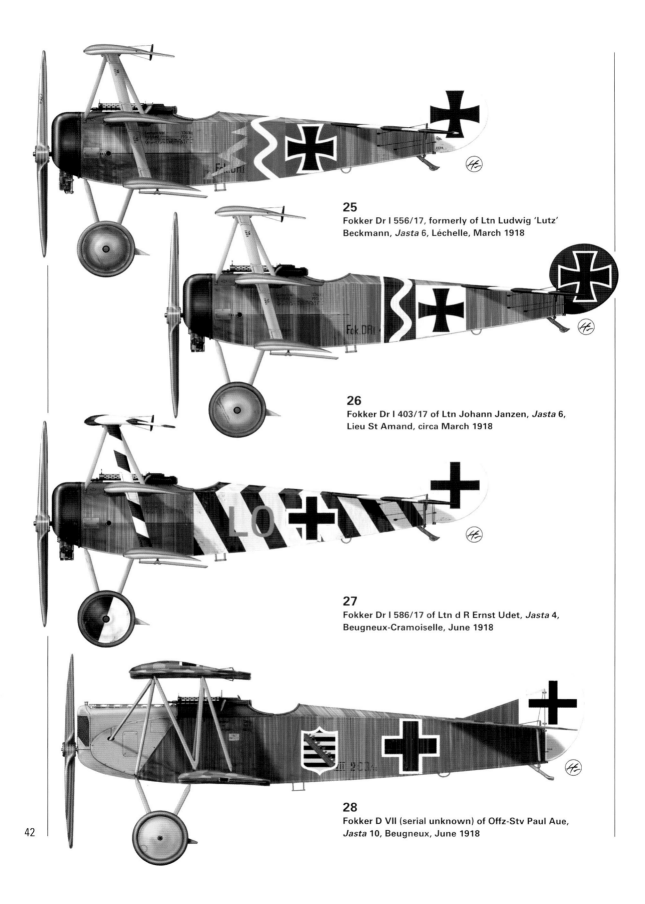

25
Fokker Dr I 556/17, formerly of Ltn Ludwig 'Lutz'
Beckmann, *Jasta* 6, Léchelle, March 1918

26
Fokker Dr I 403/17 of Ltn Johann Janzen, *Jasta* 6,
Lieu St Amand, circa March 1918

27
Fokker Dr I 586/17 of Ltn d R Ernst Udet, *Jasta* 4,
Beugneux-Cramoiselle, June 1918

28
Fokker D VII (serial unknown) of Offz-Stv Paul Aue,
Jasta 10, Beugneux, June 1918

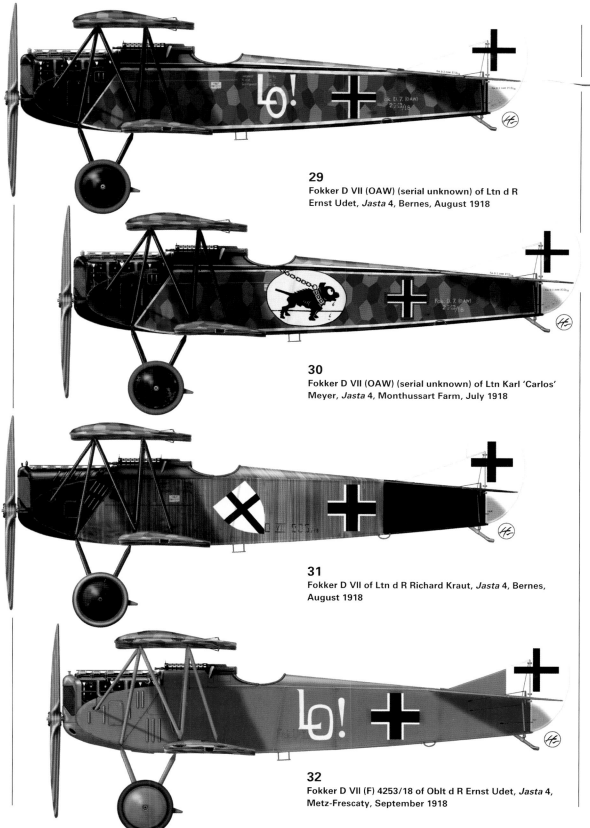

29
Fokker D VII (OAW) (serial unknown) of Ltn d R
Ernst Udet, *Jasta* 4, Bernes, August 1918

30
Fokker D VII (OAW) (serial unknown) of Ltn Karl 'Carlos'
Meyer, *Jasta* 4, Monthussart Farm, July 1918

31
Fokker D VII of Ltn d R Richard Kraut, *Jasta* 4, Bernes,
August 1918

32
Fokker D VII (F) 4253/18 of Oblt d R Ernst Udet, *Jasta* 4,
Metz-Frescaty, September 1918

43

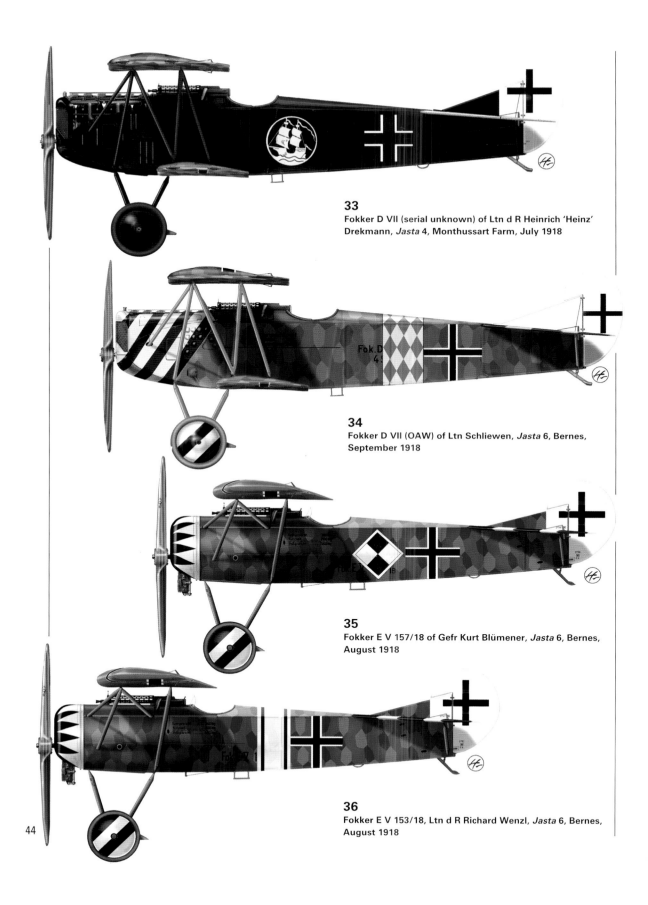

33
Fokker D VII (serial unknown) of Ltn d R Heinrich 'Heinz'
Drekmann, *Jasta* 4, Monthussart Farm, July 1918

34
Fokker D VII (OAW) of Ltn Schliewen, *Jasta* 6, Bernes,
September 1918

35
Fokker E V 157/18 of Gefr Kurt Blümener, *Jasta* 6, Bernes,
August 1918

36
Fokker E V 153/18, Ltn d R Richard Wenzl, *Jasta* 6, Bernes,
August 1918

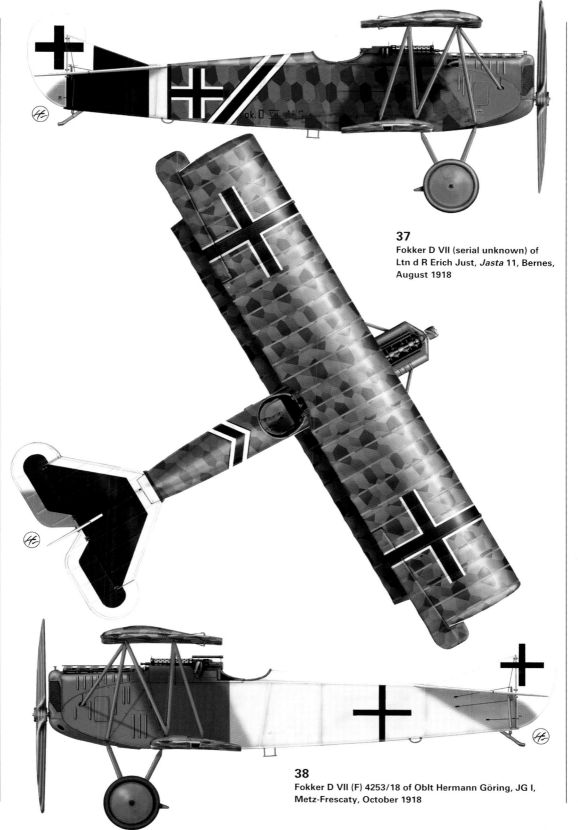

37
Fokker D VII (serial unknown) of
Ltn d R Erich Just, *Jasta* 11, Bernes,
August 1918

38
Fokker D VII (F) 4253/18 of Oblt Hermann Göring, JG I,
Metz-Frescaty, October 1918

39
Fokker D VII (serial unknown) of Ltn Hans Kirschstein,
Jasta 6, Beugneux, July 1918

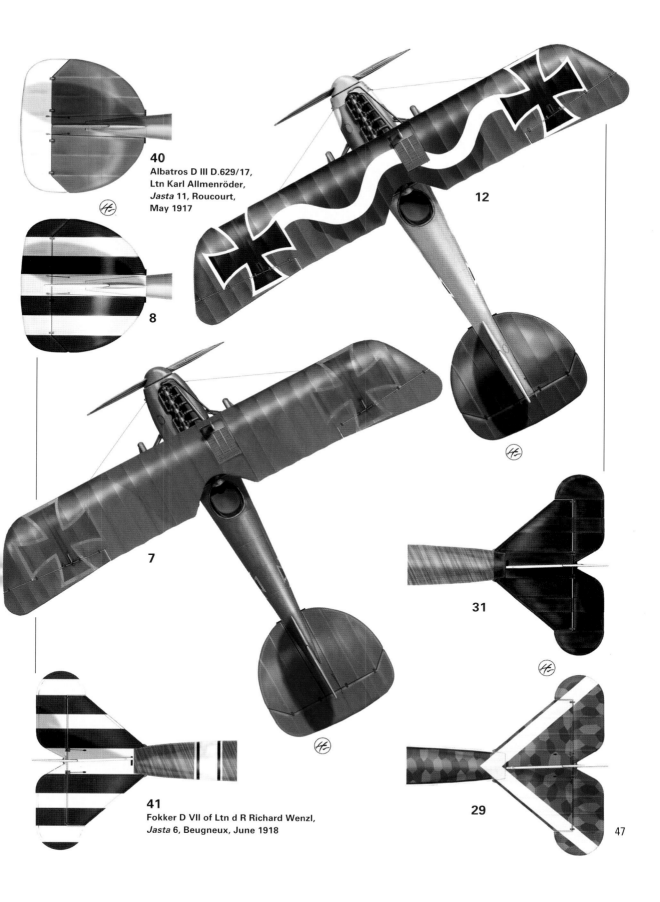

40
Albatros D III D.629/17,
Ltn Karl Allmenröder,
Jasta **11, Roucourt,**
May 1917

12

8

7

31

41
Fokker D VII of Ltn d R Richard Wenzl,
Jasta **6, Beugneux, June 1918**

29

47

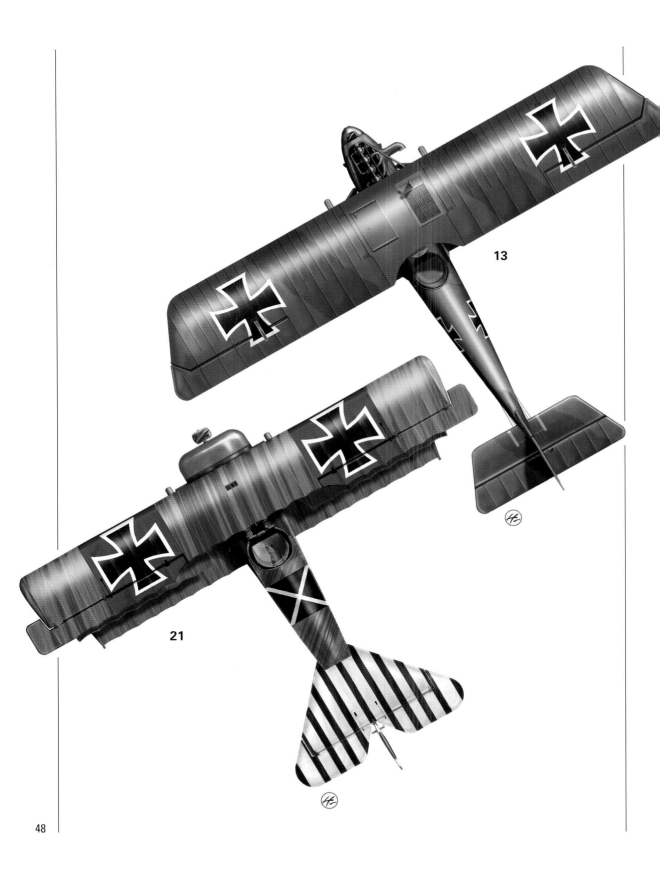

13

21

TRIPLANE TRIALS

There was an air of anticipation at JG I in late August, with the arrival of the two pre-production Fokker V 4 triplanes (F I 102/17 and 103/17) at Marckebeeke. In addition, the *Geschwader* had begun to receive its first examples of the new Pfalz D III, and these sleek silver-finished fighters generated considerable interest as well. It is believed that the first Pfalz went to *Jasta* 10, which would eventually have a full complement of the type, while others were primarily supplied to *Jasta* 4. However, the racy appearance of the Pfalz was belied by its disappointing performance – most pilots found it was not much of an improvement over the Albatros D III/V, although it was faster in a dive.

In any event, the new Fokkers garnered most of the attention. Voss had previously flown the prototype V 4 triplane at the Fokker Works in Schwerin in late June or early July, and was the first to fly the new F I 103/17 on the evening of 28 August, despite stormy weather conditions.

Anthony Fokker himself soon arrived at Marckebeeke, along with his motion picture camera, and recorded both Richthofen with 102/17 and Voss with 103/17 on film. The triplanes were soon put through their paces for a host of visiting dignitaries, including commander of the 4. *Armee* Gen Sixt von Arnim, his Chief-of-Staff Maj Gen von Lossberg, and even *Reichskanzler* Dr Michaelis.

The final days of August saw little flying activity due to poor weather. The last day of the month again dawned with low clouds and rainy skies, but these cleared sufficiently in the evening for aircraft on both sides to finally take to the air. Newly-appointed *Jasta* 6 commander Hans Adam was credited with a Sopwith near Zonnebeke at 1950 hrs.

The business end of Werner Voss' Fokker F I 103/17 of *Jagdstaffel* 10 shows off its famous facial markings. Debate still rages among enthusiasts as to whether the engine cowling of Voss' triplane was *Jasta* 10 chrome yellow or factory finish dark olive. This triplane was powered by a captured Le Rhone engine from a No 60 Sqn Nieuport 17 (*courtesy Reinhard Kastner*)

The first day of September brought the first victory for the Fokker triplane. The type was so new that its configuration would confuse both friend and foe in these early days. Flying F I 102/17, Richthofen easily dispatched an RE 8 of No 6 Sqn, its hapless crew undoubtedly mistaking the Fokker for a RNAS triplane;

'I and four gentlemen of my *Staffel* attacked a very courageously flown British artillery-spotting aircraft. Apparently the adversary had taken me for a British Triplane, as the observer stood up in his machine without making a move to attack me with his machine gun.'

A short 20 minutes later, *Jasta* 11 leader Reinhard was credited with a Sopwith single-seater near Zonnebeke for his sixth victory.

On 3 September, Monday's clear skies ushered in a day of great success. Richthofen and *Jasta* 11 again claimed the early kills at approximately

Anthony Fokker, sat in the cockpit, explains features of the new Fokker F I 102/17 to Maj Gen von Lossberg at Marckebeeke in late August 1917 – von Lossberg was Chief of the General Staff of the 4. *Armee*. Rittmeister von Richthofen is to the right of von Lossberg, and at the extreme right is probably Ltn Hans Adam of *Jasta* 6. Richthofen would score the first victories for the new aircraft when he claimed his 60th and 61st victims in the first days of September. However, Kurt Wolff would perish flying this same triplane on the 15th of that month

3 September produced a bag of ten aircraft for *Jagdgeschwader* I, including the fourth victory of Oblt Oskar Freiherr von Boenigk. The *Jasta* 4 ace is seen here in his Pfalz D III 1396/17 in the autumn of 1917. This was an early production Pfalz, marked with the *Staffel* insignia of the black ribbon wound around the fuselage. Von Boenigk apparently had the inner section of each(?) lower wing painted in a personal colour, which was probably applied to the tail as well. It is believed that this colour was most likely yellow – the colour of von Boenigk's former *Grenadier Regiment* Nr 11 *König Friedrich III*. A Silesian nobleman like the Richthofens, von Boenigk scored seven victories of his eventual 26 in *Jasta* 4

0730 hrs. Flying his new triplane 102/17, the Rittmeister led a group of Albatros fighters down on the Sopwith Pups of 'A' Flight of No 46 Sqn. Ltn Mohnicke was first to score, downing the Pup of Lt K W McDonald behind German lines – McDonald was captured, but soon died of his wounds. Richthofen had a bit more trouble bringing down Lt A F Bird, whom he acknowledged was a 'very skilful pilot' who managed to strafe an infantry column on his way down, and steered his Pup into a tree upon landing. Bird was soon taken prisoner and, to his chagrin, was filmed by Tony Fokker along with Richthofen.

About an hour later, Wüsthoff was credited with another Sopwith for his eighth kill. At 0952 hrs Voss drew his own first blood in the triplane when he claimed a No 45 Sqn Camel. Minutes after this the murderous pace continued, as *Jasta* 11 Ltns Carl-August von Schönebeck and Eberhard Stapenhörst were both credited with Sopwith Triplanes – one of these was flown by F S Lt Scott of 1 Naval Squadron, who was killed. Shortly after noon, *Jasta* 4 leader von Döring brought down his sixth – an RE 8 from the No 6 Sqn. This time the crew both survived as PoWs.

The Sopwith Triplane pilots of 1 Naval Squadron wounded Ltn d R Bockelmann of *Jasta* 11 in the leg at 1430 hrs, and he was removed to a hospital at Courtrai. Bockelmann was the only JG I casualty on this day, which was still far from over. Nineteen-year-old Kurt Wüsthoff scored for the second time at 1700 hrs with an RE 8 claimed east of Zillbeke. In the darkening evening, Hans Adam achieved his 14th victory at 1950 hrs, bagging a Nieuport of No 1 Sqn RFC. Minutes later, *Jasta* 4's von Boenigk claimed two Sopwiths, but only one was confirmed for his 4th kill, to bring the day's tally to ten aircraft credited for one pilot wounded. The following day *Jasta* 4 star Kurt Wüsthoff wrote to his mother;

'That eighth aircraft that I had shot down a while ago was later confirmed to another fellow. That is why, however, I brought down my eighth and ninth yesterday, and today my tenth and eleventh opponents. It's going especially well – my "business is booming". If it goes on this way I will soon have the *Pour le Mérite* (one gets it with 20). If I continue to have such luck, and the weather remains good, in the next few days I will be in the Army Despatches! As soon as I have the *"P le M"*, I will have leave again.'

Clearly a youngster with confidence, Wüsthoff was on a "hot streak", and he knew it. In the morning *Jasta* 4 and 11 pilots had tangled with the Pups of No 66 Sqn. Capt P G Taylor of No 66 wrote that the 12 Pups of A and C Flights of the squadron were patrolling together near Armentieres, when, 'A formation of about ten Huns, brilliantly coloured like our (old) opponents from Douai, came in from the east'. C Flight Commander Capt C C Sharpe dived to attack them, when Taylor spotted another group of enemy machines streaking down from above;

'There was immediately a violent dogfight. I saw a Pup going down, swooping in a series of dives like a falling leaf, with an Albatros circling and watching him go. About half-a-mile-away I saw a spot of flame light up in an aircraft. Only four of C Flight returned to Estrée Blanche.'

Wüsthoff probably brought down Sharpe as a PoW, and Lt S A Harper was also captured by Ltn Mohnicke of *Jasta* 11. However, Lt F A Smith succeeded in wounding Oblt Reinhard in the thigh. Reinhard made it back safely, and soon found himself as Bockelmann's roommate in

KURT WÜSTHOFF

Kurt Erwin Wüsthoff was born in Aachen on 27 January 1898 – thus he would be one of the more youthful stars of JG I. He joined the *Fliegertruppe* when still only 16½-years-old, and was posted to FEA 6 in December 1914, where he became a flying instructor. On 8 April 1916 Wüsthoff was finally sent to the Front as a pilot in *Kasta* 3 of *Kagohl* 1, and took part in aerial operations over the battlegrounds of Verdun and the Somme. He then flew bombers in campaigns in Rumania and Macedonia, but longed to fly fighters.

Wüsthoff got his wish in June 1917 when he was transferred to *Jasta* 4, and soon began his successful career. His first victory came on 15 June (a Sopwith 1½ Strutter from No 45 Sqn over Vormezeele).

An extremely ambitious and driven young man, he scored five times in July and was commissioned on 1 August. More honours and glory came his way, as he earned the 'Hohenzollern' and achieved 14 kills in September 1917. Wüsthoff received his longed-for *Pour le Mérite* on 22 November, with his tally at 26. He was the youngest airman to receive it.

However, his rapid rise to fame had come at a high personal cost. In spite of his apparent abundant confidence, he had pushed himself to his limit. Shortly after winning his 'Blue Max', Wüsthoff was sent to Dr Lahmann's Sanatorium in Dresden to recover from gastric and nervous disorders. After his return to the Front, he was appointed commander of *Jasta* 4 on 23 February 1918, at the age of 20. After his lengthy dry spell, Wüsthoff scored his 27th, and final, kill on 10 March. However, due to conflicts with his pilots and his continuing nervous problems, he was relieved of his command on 16 March 1918, as Richthofen had realised he needed a strong and respected leader in that position.

Wüsthoff was transferred to the *Geschwader* staff for a time, but he was placed at the disposal of *Idflieg* on 4 May and sent back to the Sanatorium for a time due to his nervous problems. On 16 June 1918 he returned to the Front as a pilot in *Jasta* 15, and the next day flew a patrol in the Fokker of Ltn von Hantelmann. D VII 382/18 was shot down by SE 5s of No 24 Sqn, and Wüsthoff was badly wounded in both legs and taken prisoner.

He spent the rest of the war in various French hospitals, and complained bitterly about their faulty treatment of his wounds. Wüsthoff was not released until 1920, and years of medical treatment followed to enable him to walk without crutches. He returned to flying and flew for advertising campaigns, but crashed at an airshow on 18 July 1926 and died five days later.

Vfw Kurt Erwin Wüsthoff, the ambitious and driven *Jasta* 4 ace, is seen here with an Albatros D V from his unit

Bavarian Field Hospital 133 near Courtrai. Ltn Gisbert-Wilhelm Groos took over acting command of *Jasta* 11. Reinhard would return to JG I in late November to lead *Jasta* 6.

Wüsthoff continued his impressive victory skein on the 5th, when he brought down one of the vaunted Camels at 1000 hrs for his 12th. Two of the outdated Sopwith Pups were claimed by the *Jasta* 10 team of Voss and Löwenhardt. The former was in F I 103/17, and he put on a flying exhibition for No 66 Sqn. Arthur Gould Lee of the squadron wrote;

'They were patrolling northeast of Ypres when Odell, who had seen a triplane coming down from behind, but taken no notice, thinking it was a "Nautical", was amazed to find it firing at him. He turned, then saw the black crosses. The others turned too, and a brisk little scrap followed, the Hun being joined by a D V. The triplane had a stupendous performance, and when he'd decided he'd had enough, he lifted up above everybody like a rocket. He was a pretty hot pilot, for he holed most of the Pups, but nobody could get a bead on him.'

Though 2Lt C W Odell made it back in his riddled Pup, Voss received credit for him, and the up and coming Löwenhardt received his third confirmed *Luftsieg*. Later, Voss was also credited with a 'Caudron' to bring his total to 41.

The Rittmeister was now ordered to go on a four-week recuperative leave on 6 September, in response to his flagrant disregard of orders not to fly. Von Döring again took over the post of acting *Jagdgeschwader* commander, as Oblt von Boenigk led *Jasta* 4. With Richthofen's enforced absence, the stage was clear for the mercurial Werner Voss to emerge as the premier performer of the *Geschwader*. That very day the 20-year-old flamed a FE 2d of No 20 Sqn, and he also welcomed a new pilot to *Jasta* 10 – Vfw Friedrich Rüdenberg from Hannover, a 25-year-old engineering student fresh from *Jastaschule* I. Some of Rüdenberg's letters and memoirs have recently emerged, and provide interesting details of *Jasta* 10;

'Our commander was Ltn Werner Voss – a well grown, totally fearless, rapidly comprehending and, in his conduct, very simple man. Militarily, he had the weakness of being an absolute loner. Often, he separated from his *Staffel* over the Front, and he did not train us very systematically. Our officers' mess and the quarters for some of us were in a nice small villa with a garden. Right next to it was the airfield with the hangars.'

Three days after Richthofen's leave began, JG I claimed three victories, including a balloon for Löwenhardt's fourth victory. On 10 September Voss put on a tour-de-force display as he achieved the 'hat-trick' – two

This side view of Fokker F I 103/17 displays the Fokker factory streaked camouflage, and the 'dark' finish of the cowling and wheel covers. Werner Voss blazed a bright but brief trail through the Flanders sky in September with his triplane, which was perfectly suited to his flying skills (*courtesy Reinhard Kastner*)

On 9 September 1917 *Jasta* 10 played host to a distinguished visitor – Archduke Karl-Albrecht, heir to the Austrian throne. With Richthofen on leave, it was left to acting *Geschwader* commander Oblt von Döring and *Jasta* 10 leader Werner Voss to escort the Archduke around the *Jasta* 10 airfield. Many of the well known photographs of Fokker F I 103/17 of *Jasta* 10 were taken on this occasion. Here, Voss, at right, chats with the Archduke (wearing binoculars), while second from left is von Döring. The OAW-built Albatros D III in the background was marked with a white 'snake-line' on the fuselage and upper wing. According to the late historian Heinz Nowarra (who interviewed several *Jasta* 10 personnel), this D III was the aircraft of Erich Löwenhardt, who on 9 September flamed a balloon for his fourth victory – 50 more would be added to his list before his death

No 70 Sqn Camel airmen died in front of his guns, followed shortly by a French SPAD pilot from SPA37. Voss' rampage continued the following day, as a 'new type' was claimed at 1030 hrs, and the Camel of Lt O L McMaking was sent down to crash near St Julien four hours later, ending the life of the six-victory ace from No 45 Sqn.

Voss' *Jasta* 10 comrade and administrative officer Oblt Ernst Weigand (who handled the paperwork Voss despised) also claimed a SPAD for his third opponent. Another Camel was credited to Kurt Wüsthoff, who seemed unstoppable in September – he scored again on the 12th, 13th and 15th to bring himself ever closer to his coveted *Pour le Mérite*.

VETERANS FALL

By this time Kurt Wolff of *Jasta* 11 had returned to operational flying, but without success. On the 12th he was informed by a telegram from the Kaiser that he had been promoted to oberleutnant, but this distinction failed to cheer him, as he wrote to his betrothed, 'Because, so far, I've had bad luck. I have already fought it out with about 20 Englishmen, and haven't gotten one down'. Still, his prestige remained untarnished within the *Geschwader,* and von der Osten recalled, 'He was the only one permitted to fly Richthofen's triplane during his absence, including combat flights'.

Thus it was that Wolff was flying Fokker F I 102/17 as he led a patrol of *Jasta* 11 Albatros pilots over Moorslede late in the afternoon of 15 September. They engaged a group of four Camels of 10 Naval Squadron, led by Flt Lt D F Fitzgibbon, the RNAS pilots mistakenly claiming there were five Albatros and *four* Fokker triplanes in the scrap! Flt Sub-Lt N M MacGregor reported;

'I got into a good position very close on one triplane – within 25 yard – and fired a good burst. I saw my tracers entering his machine. I next saw him going down in a vertical dive, apparently out of control.'

Fokker F I 102/17 came down near the village of Nachtigall, and the *'zarte Blümlein'* was dead. Wolff's loss was a hard blow to the *Geschwader,* and especially to Richthofen, who received the news by telegram at his parents' home in Schweidnitz. The Rittmeister wrote in Wolff's obituary, 'With his friendly nature and his quiet modesty, he was one of the dearest and best comrades to us all'. Ltn Groos was named acting commander of *Jasta* 11.

The group mourned, but only briefly – on the day after Wolff's funeral, JG I and 10 Naval Squadron tangled again. *Jasta* 6 stalwart Hans Ritter von Adam shot down the Camel of Flt Sub-Lt E Grace in flames for his 16th victory (and second of the day), while at the same time Paul Aue of *Jasta* 10 was wounded by the RNAS flight (which again included Fitzgibbon and MacGregor) over Roulers.

On 20 September, the Battle of the Menin Road Ridge (near the Ypres-Yser Canal) began, and early in the morning Martinsyde G 102 'Elephants' of No 27 Sqn bombed the *Geschwader* airfields at Marcke and Bisseghem with deadly results – five enlisted men dead, several more wounded and three aircraft of *Jasta* 4 destroyed, with six more damaged. *Geschwader* pilots were soon airborne, and seven enemy machines were claimed by day's end, with the tenacious performers Adam and Wüsthoff both achieving doubles. On the next day *Jasta* 10 was back to balloon-busting, with Ltns d R Gustav Bellen and Löwenhardt flaming one each.

Werner Voss, recently returned from a brief leave, was back in action on the 23rd. Rüdenberg later recalled, 'On the morning of 23 September, Voss returned from the Front with a loop over the field, indicating a victory'. Voss had indeed been successful in downing a DH 4 from No 57 Sqn, and its crew would be the last RFC airmen to die at Voss' hands. According to Rüdenberg, he made an ominous slip in his victory confirmation paperwork. 'When filling out the report form. He had placed his own name in line for the victim's name – he realised this and corrected it'.

Voss' brothers Otto and Max had arrived for a visit, and the three posed together for photographs. Many accounts (including one by this author) have mistakenly claimed that Voss was about to go on leave later that very day, but this is a misconception, as he had just returned from a leave.

Friedrich Rüdenberg of *Jasta* 10 sits in the cockpit of his Pfalz D III – *possibly* serial number 1371/17 (the first two numbers are obscured). This aircraft displayed the chrome yellow nose, struts and wheel covers of *Jasta* 10, with Rüdenberg's personal stripe markings on the fuselage and tail. In the distance is the Pfalz probably flown by Hans Klein, with a lengthwise stripe along the fuselage. Rüdenberg was one of two *Staffel* pilots who took off with Voss on his last flight on 23 September, but who soon became separated from the *Staffelführer*. On 11 November Rüdenberg was posted to *Idflieg*, but would fly again with *Jasta* 75 in 1918

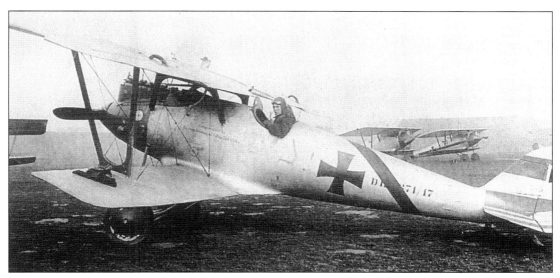

At about 1800 hrs Voss took off for an evening patrol in his triplane, accompanied by Bellen and Rüdenberg – both in Pfalz D IIIs. It is believed a second *Jasta* 10 *Kette* (flight) left shortly thereafter, led by Weigand. However, as Rüdenberg wrote his brother;

'I told you that he (Voss) flew a special machine that did not allow us to catch up with him. When he attacked a single-seater, our cover of his rear was missing, and fate took its course. The single German triplane was attacked from all sides because every Englishman could figure out that it did not contain a beginner.'

In his superb triplane, Voss had again outdistanced his *Kette.* The story of the epic combat that followed has been told many times.

Two flights of No 60 Sqn were returning home, with 'A' Flight having been reduced to just two SE 5s, flown by Capts Hamersley and R L Chidlaw-Roberts. Hamersley was attacked by Voss and severely shot up. Chidlaw-Roberts would recall many years later;

'The triplane then went for Hamersley and his (Hamersley's) machine was soon going down pouring smoke. I fired at Voss, but before I could do much he was on my tail and had shot about my rudder. I realised that I'd met somebody I couldn't handle, and the sooner I got home, the better. So I got in a spin and that's when No 56 Sqn came along. I was jolly glad they did.'

The timely intervention was by 'B' Flight of No 56 Sqn, which consisted of seven veteran pilots led by the redoubtable J T B McCudden. A P F Rhys-Davids attacked Voss from the left and McCudden from the right, but Voss turned in what a startled McCudden termed 'a sort of flat half spin'. Voss dazzled and outfought 'B' Flight for several minutes, hitting every SE 5. For a few minutes he was joined by an unknown pilot in a red-nosed Albatros, by which time Voss had already so damaged the machines of K K Muspratt and V P Cronyn that they were forced to escape and try to reach their airfield. The Albatros eventually disappeared, but Voss stayed to battle it out. G H Bowman recalled;

'We were then at about 2000 ft – at that altitude Voss had a much better rate of climb, or rather zoom, than we had, and frequently he was the highest machine of the seven. He could have turned east and got away had he wished to, but he was not that type, and always came down on us again.'

Finally, though, Rhys-Davids got on to Voss' tail and fired a telling burst. McCudden saw Voss in his final moments. 'He was very low, still being engaged by an SE marked "I", the pilot being Rhys-Davids. I noticed that the triplane's movements were very erratic, and then I saw it hit the ground.'

That evening, worries beset the *Geschwader* when Voss failed to return. According to Rüdenberg;

'At night we received news from our first (front) line about an aerial fight between one German and six Englishman – the German crashed. The next morning we all flew over the Front and dropped a letter with a long black-white-red banner requesting notification about the fate of Voss.'

On the same 24 September, Ltn d R Rudolf Wendelmuth of *Jasta* 8 reported that Voss had been pursuing a 'Sopwith' (a word Germans often used for SE 5s) when he was shot down from behind by another, and that his machine crashed north of Frezenberg, behind the enemy lines. At any rate, Voss was buried where he fell in the battle-torn landscape, without ceremony, by gunners of 174 Brigade, Royal Field Artillery, 58th Division, under the command of Lt Keegan.

Oblt Weigand took over as acting CO of *Jasta* 10, and on 25 September Lothar von Richthofen arrived to resume command of *Jasta* 11.

Still more misfortune came to the 'yellow nose' *Staffel* that same day, however. As Weigand led a four-aircraft sortie over the Houthulst Forest, a single SE 5 pilot left his formation to make an audacious attack on the German scouts, shooting down two of the *Jasta* 10 machines. Rüdenberg's memoirs are a bit confused in regard to the details of this event, but he did retain an accurate impression of the RFC airman;

'An exemplary fighter pilot. He was a loner. In his first attack he descended in a steep dive, and with a few bursts from his two machine guns, he shot down Weigand out our midst. The English pilot obviously was a master shot.'

In the space of a few minutes, *Jasta* 10 lost its acting commander Weigand and newly-arrived Uffz August Werkmeister to this remarkable display by Lt Barlow of No 56 Sqn – both German aircraft fell in flames.

Having lost two commanders in two days, *Jasta* 10 would now be led by Hans Klein (the former *Jasta* 4 star), who had recovered from his wound of July. As the Allied ground attacks in the Third Battle of Ypres intensified, heavy fog and rains limited *Geschwader* operations.

On 3 October Klein opened his *Jasta* 10 book with a DH 4 of No 55 Sqn, but on the same patrol Rüdenberg made an emergency landing due to lack of fuel, writing off his fighter, and Ltn d R Max Römer was downed in flames. Rüdenberg later claimed that Römer had been attacked by another German pilot who was unfamiliar with the lines of the new Pfalz D III the *Jasta* 10 pilot was flying. Further bad weather curtailed flying for two weeks, but the hard-hit *Jasta* 10 was back in action on the 18th, with Klein and Löwenhardt both claiming Bristols. RFC bombing raids struck the *Geschwader* airfields on 21 and 22 October, inflicting limited damage.

Following the death of Oblt Weigand on 25 September, *Jasta* 10 was placed in the capable hands of Ltn d R Hans Klein, who had achieved 16 victories with *Jasta* 4. He is standing in the centre of this group beneath the chrome yellow nose of the Pfalz D III which is believed to be his aircraft. It was marked with a lengthwise stripe along the fuselage, seemingly of the same yellow colour as the nose – the tail was over-painted as well

Dr I STRUCTURAL FAILURES

The melancholy mood which permeated the *Geschwader* may have lifted a bit on the 23rd when the Rittmeister returned from his leave to resume full command, which coincided with the recent arrival of 17 of the new Fokker Dr I aircraft at Marckebeeke. In spite of the losses of Voss and Wolff in triplanes, the new machines were still welcomed with great anticipation by *Jasta* 11.

However, bad luck and faulty construction would plague the aircraft. On 29 October Vfw Lautenschlager was accidentally killed by a German airman who mistook his Dr I 113/17 for a Sopwith Triplane, and the following day both Lothar and Manfred von Richthofen suffered forced landings in their triplanes, Manfred's 114/17 being damaged. The worst came on the succeeding day, however, when Ltn d R Günther Pastor crashed fatally in Dr I 121/17 due to the structural collapse of his upper wing. This tragedy, combined with the death of Heinrich Gontermann of *Jasta* 15 due to a similar failure, led to the immediate grounding of all Fokker triplanes at the Front.

An *Idflieg* crash committee investigated the Dr I, and discovered that the ailerons would detach under the loading imposed by steep banks or side-slips due to faulty attachment points. Glue joints in the Dr I's upper wings were found to have been weakened by condensation within the wings – all this indicated poor workmanship and inferior quality control at the Fokker factory. Fokker was ordered to carry out various modifications and inspections on all triplane airframes. Strengthened wings and redesigned ailerons were hastily fitted.

Thus, the beleaguered airmen of JG I were forced to make do with their mediocre Albatros and Pfalz fighters. This hardly seems to have bothered the enterprising Kurt Wüsthoff of *Jasta* 4, who continued 'his string of destruction'. On 27 October, Wüsthoff shot up a Sopwith 'Tripe' for his 22nd victory. The next day he wrote to his mother, listing the scores of his competitors and his imagined 'place' in his rankings of the living German aces;

The Fokker Dr I's similarity to the Sopwith Triplane could act both in favour of and against its pilots in the early days of its deployment. On 29 October 1917, *Jasta* 11 pilot Vfw Josef Lautenschlager's Dr I 113/17 was accidentally shot down by a pilot from another *Jagdstaffel,* and it crashed north of Houthulst Forest. The Dr I had arrived at Marckebeeke as part of the initial shipment of 17 triplanes around nine days earlier

The funeral of Vfw Josef Lautenschlager was held at 1500 hrs on 3 November 1917. The marker reveals that he was born on 12 March 1892 in Reifenthal, in Bavaria. As was often the custom, this airman's grave was marked with a scrap propeller

On the last day of October, Ltn Günther Pastor of *Jasta* 11 was killed when his Fokker Dr I 121/17 crashed due to structural failure of the top wing. Together with the loss of Heinrich Gontermann of *Jasta* 15 the previous day, this resulted in the grounding of the type until an investigation could be carried out. In *Jasta* 11 it was the custom to paint out most of the white national insignia field with solid olive to produce the regulation five-centimetre white border, and this was already in effect on this Dr I

'Ltn v Bülow received the *Pour le Mérite* for his 21st. I hope to get it very soon, too! Oblt Schleich, Oblt Berthold, wounded. Now I'm the one at the Front. I am in excellent spirits.'

On the last day of the month he despatched an SE 5 of No 84 Sqn, followed by a pair of Camels on 5 November. On the 6th the Canadian Corps took their objective of Passchendaele – two *Jasta* 6 pilots braved the wind and rain to bring down two British aircraft. Wüsthoff claimed an RE 8 on the 9th to bring his tally to 26, and on the same day Lothar von Richthofen returned to the lists by downing a Bristol Fighter for his 25th.

On 15 November the skies cleared a bit and action intensified. By that evening, the mood in the *Geschwader* officers' mess was once again strained and grim – the highly decorated *Jasta* 6 commander Hans Ritter von Adam, victor in 21 air combats, lay dead near the wreckage of his Albatros D V 5222/17 northwest of Kortewilde. He had been shot down by British fighters at 0920 hrs. German intelligence officer Hans Schröder wrote;

'Adam's body was not discovered at once. They found the wreckage of his machine, but no corpse. Then, three days later, the body was found –

The black ribbon painted around its fuselage identifies this Pfalz D IIIa as a Jasta 4 machine. The black chordwise stripes on the fin, elevators and horizontal stabilisers were the unknown pilot's personal markings. Strong sunlight has apparently washed out the cross insignia on the rudder

The pilot of *Jasta* 6 Albatros D Va 5237/17 runs up the engine as one mechanic holds down the tail and another stands ready at the wing tip – unfortunately, more details about this photograph are lacking. The D Va displayed the black and white zebra striping so characteristic of this unit on its rear fuselage and tail, and the pilot's intriguing personal chevron band was marked on the fuselage. The wings were covered in five-colour fabric (*HAC/UTD*)

stark naked – behind a bush. Things had come to such a pitch that our own men could rob a dead German hero of the air of his clothing.'

On the 20th, Adam's body was taken to the train station at Courtrai for the trip home – a familiar experience for the airmen who accompanied the cortege.

THE TANK BATTLE OF CAMBRAI

The staff of JG I had already begun planning for a move to the 2. *Armee* Front by mid-November, but events outpaced them with unexpected fury. On 20 November the British First and Third Armies launched the Battle of Cambrai. Disdaining the typical pre-offensive barrage, they unleashed 381 tanks against the German lines between Gonnelieu and Havrincourt, followed by waves of infantry and low-flying RFC airmen who braved the heavy fog and low clouds. They broke through the German lines with shocking success. Against some 289 RFC aircraft, the 2. *Armee* possessed only 78 machines, and only one fighter unit (*Jasta* 5) at Estourmel. Bodenschatz wrote;

'The *Jagdgeschwader* is being hurled at the endangered Front, and they depart in frantic haste – everybody else is to follow immediately by rail. Immediately? Cars and vehicles are scarcely to be had at all, and the railways are jammed full of troops.'

Amidst the confusion and bad weather, *Jasta* 11 and the Group Staff were eventually relocated to Avesnes-le-Sec, *Jagdstaffeln* 4 and 6 moved to Lieu St Amand and *Jasta* 10 transferred to Iwuy – all four *Staffeln* being located within five kilometres of each other. Richthofen would assume overall command of all of the *Jastas* which had been rushed to the area.

Even before the entire *Geschwader* was in place, the Rittmeister was back in the air on the 23rd. He led a combined group from JG I and elements of *Jastas* 5 and 15 on a patrol over Bourlon Wood (which was taken that day by the British 51st Division). In his Albatros D V 4693/17, with its red cowling and tail, he attacked a DH 5 of No 64 Sqn north of Fontaine-Notre-Dame and it fell into the southeast corner of the Wood as his 62nd victim. At the same time Lothar brought down a Bristol F 2B for his 26th kill, and Ltn d R Kurt Küppers of *Jasta* 6 achieved 'acedom' with a 'Sopwith' (perhaps another No 64 Sqn DH 5) at 1500 hrs.

The flurry of organisational activity continued, and the *Staffeln* were entirely settled in the new locations by the 25th. Two days later there was no flying, but the long-awaited telegram arrived for Kurt Wüsthoff, conferring the coveted 'Blue Max' on the teenager. However, the intense pressures experienced in reaching this goal had taken their toll on him, and he was soon sent to a sanatorium in Dresden for increasing stomach ailments and a nervous disorder.

On 29 November, three aircraft fell to the *Geschwader* pilots, including Klein's 21st, putting him in line for his own *Pour le Mérite* telegram.

Over the battlefront, the increased activity of German artillery-spotting and reconnaissance aircraft indicated that a counter-attack was in preparation. The official RAF historian wrote, 'In the southern area some anxiety was caused by the appearance of many low-flying German aircraft, among which the coloured aeroplanes of the Richthofen "Circus" were said to be conspicuous'.

The counter-attack was launched at 0700 hrs on 30 November, which proved to be a day of furious action for JG I with 103 sorties being flown. Hans Klein flamed a British balloon at 1230 hrs for his 22nd victory, and celebrated his award of the 'Blue Max' later that day. In the afternoon five aircraft were sent hurtling to earth by *Geschwader* pilots, including the Rittmeister (63rd victory). Hans-Georg von der Osten wrote;

'On 30 November, with the cloud ceiling at only 400 metres, I managed to shoot down one DH 5 out of a group which had suddenly appeared out of the clouds above. It crashed into the shell-torn ground south of Bourlon Wood. Immediately after the landing, Richthofen congratulated me, but at the same time rebuked me because after my first attack I had not followed the crippled aircraft into the first turn. I had had to turn away because of the attack of another Britisher who, as we used to say in frontline German "was spitting into my crate from behind". I mention this to show how closely Richthofen watched over the whole battle scene.'

Two JG I pilots were lost that day, but there was little time to dwell on their deaths. Rüdenberg summed up their fatalistic attitude;

'It just happened, and one did not make too much of it. During a meal one of us stopped his soup spoon on its way to his mouth and said that none of us would have more than nine months. "Maybe so", said another, and we continued eating.'

December's wintry weather made flying all the more difficult. On the 4th the group flew 55 sorties, but three *Jasta* 11 pilots damaged their Albatros D Vs in poor landings. The next day brought the first victories for Vfw Adam Barth of *Jasta* 10, and a promising newcomer to *Jasta* 4, Ltn Egon Koepsch, a Silesian and a former Uhlan. The Battle of Cambrai ended on 7 December, but JG I pilots continued patrols despite the worsening weather. Another new name appeared in the victory log on

Ltn Aloys Heldmann is helped with his flying gear as his Pfalz D III (1395/17) awaits. This was one of the early Pfalz D III examples that left the factory with a terrain camouflage (probably in green and a mauve or lilac) adorning its uppersurfaces. The wheels of this machine were a very pale colour, being either white or light blue. Heldmann is reported as having achieved his third victory of 29 November in Pfalz D III 4117/17, marked with a yellow nose and blue elevator. His fourth victory of 9 March 1918 was attained in Albatros D Va 5401/17, also marked with 'blue elevators'

This classic view of *Jasta* 10's Pfalz D IIIs on the field at Marcke was copied from mechanic Karl Timm's album by historian Alex Imrie. These Pfalz uniformly display the unit's chrome yellow colour on their noses, wheel covers and struts, although differing colours could be applied to the fuselage and tails as personal insignia. Second from left is D.1384/17 with a dark tail, and fifth from left is the D III believed to be Klein's machine. Seventh from left is Rüdenberg's Pfalz and eighth in line is Vfw Hecht's D III 1370/17, marked with two black fuselage bands and a green tail. Hecht landed behind British lines in this D III on 27 December 1917, which was subsequently given the British number 'G 110' (*Alex Imrie via HAC/UTD*)

the 12th when Ltn d R Erich Just of *Staffel* 11 achieved his initial kill (a balloon) of six. Three days later it was von der Osten's turn;

'The downing of an SE 5a on 15 December near Havrincourt took place at long range, as I could not overtake the enemy aeroplane which was much faster. I fired, emptying both my machine guns at him, and then saw my opponent touch down in a crash-landing. These SE 5s were our nastiest opponents due to their speed and climbing ability.'

Such realisations gave the *Geschwader* pilots all the more reason to welcome the arrival of the first consignment of Fokker Dr Is with strengthened and modified wings in late December. Enough arrived for *Jasta* 11 to be completely re-equipped by early January, and *Jasta* 6 also received a full complement of triplanes – both units would retain some Albatros biplanes, and flew both types until February. *Jasta* 4 would belatedly attain triplanes on 20 April, but *Jasta* 10 had to persevere with the Albatros and Pfalz.

It was in Pfalz D III 1370/17 that Vzfw Hecht (*Jasta* 10) had landed behind British lines on 27 December after a fight with a two-seater. Hecht was taken prisoner and his Pfalz became the subject of technical scrutiny. That same day a *Jasta* 11 pilot crashed to his death in an Albatros, but there were few other noteworthy events in the last weeks of 1917, as the winter lull set in. Manfred and Lothar von Richthofen spent Christmas with their father at the Front, but were soon on their way to Brest-Litovsk to witness the peace negotiations with the defeated Russian delegation.

1918 BEGINS

With limited hostile aircraft activity during the winter, some *Geschwader* airmen resumed balloon hunting. *Jasta* 10's resident 'gas bag' specialist, Erich Löwenhardt, set another one ablaze on the 5th for his ninth kill. On 13 January two *Jasta* 11 pilots also went 'sausage' hunting in their new triplanes. Ltn Werner Steinhäuser achieved the first combat success for the Dr I (as opposed to the earlier F Is) when he burned a balloon near Heudicourt. However, his wingman Eberhard Stapenhorst had to make a forced landing when his Dr I 144/17 was hit by anti-aircraft fire, and RFC intelligence was presented with another example of a new German fighter to study.

Five days later, Löwenhardt was credited with a two-seater to bring him into the ranks of the ten-victory *Kanonen*. On the 30th, his *Jasta* 10 comrade Adam Barth was killed when his D V 4565/17 was shot down in a solo attack by McCudden of No 56 Sqn.

The promising career of Ltn Eberhard Stapenhorst was cut short on 13 January 1918 when his Dr I 144/17 was brought down by anti-aircraft fire during an attack on a British balloon at Heudecourt. Although his companion Ltn Steinhäuser was successful in destroying the captive balloon, Stapenhorst became a PoW. He had joined *Jasta* 11 on 30 June 1917 and achieved four victories in August and September

Fokker Dr I 144/17 was brought down behind British lines on 13 January 1918 and its pilot, Ltn Stapenhorst, made a PoW. This Dr I was one of a batch of ten triplanes despatched to *Jasta* 11 on 12 December 1917, and these had asymmetrical ailerons fitted possibly to enhance the aircraft's rate of roll to the right. This Fokker became the subject of intense technical scrutiny, and reports on it were eventually published in *Flight* magazine. Stapenhorst's personal marking was the black and white chequerboard band on the fuselage. No mention is made of the colour of the cowling in any of the reports on this aircraft, and it is assumed it had not been painted red at this point

In the grim grey skies of February 1918, JG I achieved but a single victory, and the *Geschwader* war diary monotonously repeats the phrases, 'No special occurrences. Overcast, fog'. On the 17th Ltn Friedrich-Wilhelm Lübbert of *Jasta* 11 (whose brother Eduard had died as the *Jasta's* first casualty almost a year before) was seriously wounded in the arm by an SE 5. Two days later the group suffered a greater loss when the stalwart

Jasta 10 pilot Vfw Adam Barth was happy to pose with his reluctant guests Sgt Everix and Lt Whitworth of No 11 Sqn. On 5 December Barth scored his first, and only, confirmed victory when he brought down their Bristol Fighter A7143. A longtime member of *Jasta* 10, Barth would be killed in Albatros D V 4565/17 on 30 January 1918, shot down near Anneux

An unidentified pilot from *Jasta* 10 poses with one of the unit's Pfalz D IIIas, marked with the usual yellow nose, struts and wheel covers. The D IIIa differed from the D III in the fact that its machine guns were mounted on top of the fuselage ahead of the cockpit, and were not buried within the fuselage as with the D III – a tailplane of greater area was also fitted. The tail of this D IIIa may have been painted white (*courtesy F Hallensleben via P Kilduff*)

Using gestures familiar to fighter pilots of any generation, *Jasta* 4 commander Kurt Wüsthoff (left) shows an amused Karl 'Carlos' Meyer 'how it's done' in this view taken at Lieu St Amand airfield in February 1918. The Albatros D Va bore five-colour lozenge fabric on its wings and the usual *Jasta* 4 spiral black ribbon. Wüsthoff may have been displaying a little more bravado than he felt, as he had already made one trip to a Dresden sanatorium for stomach problems and a nervous disorder, and he had not scored since 9 November. Wüsthoff would enjoy aerial success only once more, on 10 March, and six days later Richthofen relieved him of his command due to his nervous problems and conflicts with his men. The Venezuelan-born Meyer had already served in *Jagdstaffeln* 11 and 4 for months when this photograph was taken, and had been wounded the previous July

Jasta 10 leader Hans Klein landed in Pfalz D IIIa 4283/17 and clambered out 'greatly upset'. He had received a glancing shot to his right arm and his right index finger had been shot off – he was sent to hospital and would not return to operational flying.

Having returned to the Front, Kurt Wüsthoff was given acting leadership of *Jasta* 4 (as von Döring went on leave) on the 10th, and became the official commander on the 23rd. On the last day of February, preparations for the much-anticipated March Offensive got underway as work commenced on constructing an advanced landing field at Awoingt.

The March Offensive would be Germany's last great gamble for victory – a titanic effort which had its origins in the defeat of Russia. The Eastern Front armistice went into effect on 3 March 1918, releasing thousands of battle-hardened troops for the West. The British blockade had brought severe hardship on the German home front, and the commitment of

Germany's allies Austria-Hungary, Turkey and Bulgaria was shaky at best. The huge manpower reserves and industrial contributions of the United States would only worsen the situation for Germany as time passed. Therefore it was imperative for Gens Hindenburg and Ludendorff to achieve a quick military victory in the west before the might of the United States could be brought to bear. Ludendorff planned to accomplish this through a massive attack against the British Fifth and Third Armies.

The sense of anticipation and intense preparation for the 'push' raised the spirits of the JG I pilots as the March weather improved, and *Jasta* 11 began to achieve something like its old panache and form. Manfred and Lothar von Richthofen had both returned to the unit, and by 10 March the *Geschwader* had noticed an increase in enemy air activity as RFC reconnaissance machines attempted to gather intelligence on the build-up for the coming offensive.

That day also saw the third victory of a fast-rising *Jasta* 6 pilot, Vfw Franz Hemer. Before the war he had been an accomplished concert cellist, and was known as 'Locken' to his comrades because of his curly blonde hair. Since 9 March, *Jastas* 4 and 10 had been assigned to fly sorties in the neighbouring 6. *Armee* area, and on the 12th they contributed three to the *Geschwader* total of seven victories for the day, including Wüsthoff's 28th, and final, victory. The Richthofen brothers were clearly back in business, with two Bristol F 2Bs falling to Lothar and another to Manfred, as *Jasta* 11 decimated a formation of No 62 Sqn aircraft late that morning. However, the next day – the unlucky 13th – would again prove ill-fated for Lothar.

The day's combat was typical of the ever-increasing scale of the frequent contests between fleets of aircraft as the offensive drew near. A massed formation of JG I fighters, led by the Rittmeister in Dr I 152/17, attacked 11 of their previous day's opponents – No 62 Sqn Bristol Fighters. They were escorting DH 4 bombers from two squadrons, and two flights of No 73 Sqn Camels waded into the fray as well, as did aircraft from *Jasta* 56. One of the Bristol pilots involved, Capt G F Hughes, said;

'By far the most amazing fight I ever had beyond description. I have never seen anything like the tracers that streaked the air from the triplanes that were round our tail in a semi-circle.'

Manfred von Richthofen busily despatched one of the Camels, as did *Jasta* 11's Edgar Scholz. The Rittmeister did not witness his brother's

Ltn d R Erich Bahr of *Jasta* 11 poses with one of the unit's triplanes in the winter of 1917-18, probably at Avesnes-le-Sec – the cowling of the fighter may have been painted red by this time. Bahr was posted to *Jasta* 11 on 27 November 1917, and the 24-year-old was killed when his Dr I (106/17) was shot down on at 1040 hrs on 6 March between Nauroy and Etricourt

Lieu St Amand airfield was the setting for this shot of Ltn d R Skauraudzun of *Jasta* 4 in February 1918, with a well-decorated Albatros D V in the background. The unusual (for *Jasta* 4) display of a 'W' on the fuselage and the black(?) and white décor on the tail and wheel covers indicates that this D V was *probably* flown by *Staffelführer* Kurt Wüsthoff. Wüsthoff had used similar tail colours on his previous Albatros D III (*OAW*)

Jagdstaffel 11 lost its commander on 13 March 1918 when Lothar von Richthofen's Dr I 454/17 suffered failure of the leading edge of its top wing during combat with Bristol Fighters of No 62 Sqn and Camels from No 73 Sqn at a height of 4000 metres. Lothar struggled to retain control of his crippled triplane as he guided it down near Awoingt, and he was close to the ground when he tried to turn to avoid some high-tension wires and crashed badly. This Dr I had Lothar's light yellow colour applied on the rear fuselage and tail, and thinly on the upper wing as well. The ace sustained severe maxillofacial injuries in the crash, and would not return to *Jasta* 11 until July

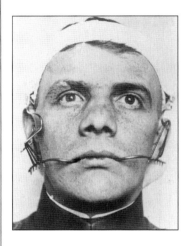

Hardly the image of the devil-may-care fighter pilot, Lothar von Richthofen simply looks like a young man in a good deal of pain in this photograph, taken during his convalescence from injuries sustained on 13 March 1918. His broken jaw is wired and his nose was broken as well. Note the injury to the right eye, which would continue to trouble him during his return to combat flying in the summer

triplane suffer leading-edge failure of the top wing, and go plummeting out of the fight with pieces of the wing tearing away. Whether the damage to the triplane's wing was incurred through stressful manoeuvres or British fire remains uncertain. Lothar managed to regain some control as he neared the ground, but he crashed badly. The resultant injuries to his eye, nose and jaw kept him out of action until the summer.

Once he knew his brother was safe in a field hospital, the Rittmeister returned to the responsibilities of preparing for the offensive. On 16 March he had the unpleasant duty of replacing the commander of *Jasta* 4. As von der Osten later recalled;

'Ltn Wüsthoff was a most dashing and successful fighter pilot. He had been assigned command of *Jasta* 4. I heard that they did not like him much there. He was the youngest – very much younger than all his pilots – and he had a very cheeky way. Apart from not being a very sympathetic man, he reported victories he did not always check. So von Richthofen relieved him as *Staffel* leader. I became his successor.'

Apart from these concerns, Richthofen was certainly aware that Wüsthoff's nerves were still in tatters. Wüsthoff was transferred to the JG I staff, and soon left the *Geschwader* altogether.

'A DAY OF GLORY'

With the massive offensive imminent, Richthofen's eager pilots – many flying the Fokker Dr I – had reached their peak of fighting efficiency and coordination at precisely the right time. This was amply demonstrated in the massive dogfight of 18 March, which became known as 'The Air Battle of Le Cateau'. Bodenschatz called it 'a day of glory for *Jagdgeschwader* I'.

Just before 1030 hrs, forward observers alerted JG I and other *Jastas* that a large formation of British aircraft was heading toward Busigny. It was comprised of DH 4 bombers of 5 Naval Squadron, escorted by higher groups of 12 Camels from No 54 Sqn and 18 SE 5s from No 84 Sqn – No 11 Sqn Bristols would also join in. One of the DH 4 pilots was Flt Cdr C Bartlett, who wrote that the whole idea was 'to clear the enemy right out of the sky', with the DH 4s acting as bait.

Soon the Rittmeister led 30 fighters into the steel blue skies, his own Dr I at the head of *Jasta* 11, with *Jasta* 6's triplanes 600 metres above on

Ltn d R Joschkowitz (left) scans the sky for signs of enemy aircraft from Lieu St Amand airfield in February 1918, while Ltn 'Carlos' Meyer smiles for the camera. Joschkowitz scored but a single victory – a SPAD on 26 September 1917. Even during the great Spring Offensive JG I maintained high standards, and after serving for seven months in *Jasta* 4, Joschkowitz was posted out to *Armee Flug Park* 2 on 1 April 1918. Meyer attained four victories in *Jastas* 11 and 4

his left, and *Jasta* 10 to his right. At a height of about 5300 metres, the German wedge knifed into the RFC formation. Richthofen wrote that he spattered a trailing two-seater with a burst, but let his *Staffel* mate Gussmann finish it off;

'After that, I gathered my 30 aircraft, climbed to 5300 metres and followed two British groups that had broken through toward Le Cateau. When the enemy attempted to turn away and head back toward the Front, I attacked him in the vicinity of Le Cateau. Meanwhile, my *Staffel* was embroiled in a bitter dogfight with enemy single-seater formations, which suddenly swooped down.'

More German fighters from *Jagdgruppen* 2, 9 and 10 were also pulled into the swirling melee and, 'A chaotic muddle of individual combats was the result'. At the end of the confusing and far-ranging dogfight, nine aircraft were credited to JG I pilots for the loss of *Jasta* 10 neophyte Flgr Rudolf Ihde. The veterans Richthofen, Reinhard, Löwenhardt and Scholz

A thinly-applied white fuselage band identified the Dr I (possibly 568/17) of Ltn d R Robert Tüxen of *Jagdstaffel* 6. The aircraft shows off the classic black and white tail stripes of the *Staffel* and the distinctive Fokker streaked camouflage. This Dr I would also have had the black cowling characteristic of *Jasta* 6 triplanes (*HAC/UTD*)

Here is Ltn Tüxen, all suited up and ready to go in his *Jasta* 6 Dr I (probably 568/17). Barely visible at left is the rectangular access panel just forward of the carburettor air intake tube – another characteristic of *Jasta* 6 triplanes. The heavy staining on the fuselage was common to all Dr Is after some time in service (*HAC/UTD*)

The pilot of this *Jasta* 11 Dr I has been incorrectly identified by some (this author included) as Vfw Edgar Scholz, but it is now believed that it is in fact Ltn Hans Joachim Wolff. Having survived previous wounds and injury, '*Wölffchen*' really came into his own flying the triplane, scoring ten victories in two months in the spring of 1918. The fuselage band painted ahead of the national insignia was certainly in yellow – the colour of Wolff's old Uhlan regiment. Wolff was one of the last pilots to see Richthofen's triplane in flight on 21 April, and he would follow his idol the Rittmeister in death on 6 May

added to their tallies, while Hans Joachim Wolff of *Jasta* 11 and Ltn Hans Kirschstein of *Jasta* 6 began their stellar careers with their initial *Luftsieg* this day. Every one of the British units involved lost aircraft. No 54 Sqn was decimated, losing five pilots killed or captured. Bartlett recalled;

'I was talking over the 'phone to Capt Kitto, No 54 Sqn's leader, and he said it was by far the biggest scrap he had ever been in. He seemed quite unnerved, and kept repeating, "Frightful affair". Undoubtedly, the Germans concentrated their forces, including Richthofen's startlingly-coloured "Circus". Many of them were really full-out, and put up a good show, particularly the Fokker triplanes.'

It was a dress rehearsal for the great aerial battles to come. In the afternoon and evening of 20 March, the entire *Geschwader* made the stealthy move to the advance landing field at Awoingt, which had been prepared as secretly as possible for the past eight nights. The aircraft were shoved into tent hangars, and that evening Richthofen briefed his *Staffel* leaders of the orders for the Offensive. All was ready.

KAISERSCHLACHT

At 0445 hrs in the morning on 21 March 1918, 10,000 German artillery pieces opened fire along a 70-kilometre-wide fog-bound front in the sectors of the German 17., 2. and 18. *Armees*. In five hours they expended 1,160,000 shells in a bombardment unsurpassed until 1945. At about 0940 hrs, Gen Ludendorff's assault troops advanced through thick fog and behind a creeping barrage to attack the British Third and Fifth Armies. The great German Spring Offensive, called the *Kaiserschlacht* (Emperor's Battle) by Ludendorff, had begun.

2. *Armee Kofl* Hptm Haehnelt had made Richthofen responsible for aerial action in 'Zone North', an area stretching from Marcoing to Venduille. The Rittmeister was given the leadership of *Jagdgruppe* 2 (*Jagdstaffeln* 5 and 46), in addition to JG I. 'Zone South' was to receive the attention of JGr 9 and 10, thus placing about 150 fighters in readiness for the 2. *Armee*.

On 20 March (the eve of the great Spring Offensive, which commenced on the 21st) the aircraft of the *Geschwader* were moved to the advance landing ground at Awoingt as secretly as possible. They are seen at this site during the *Kaiserschlacht*. At right are yellow-nosed Pfalz D IIIa and Albatros machines of *Jasta* 10, and in the distance at left are a similar mixed group of *Jasta* 4 aircraft, marked with the unit's spiral band emblem

Friedrich 'Fritz' Friedrichs of *Jasta* 10 started off his impressive career as a 'balloon-buster' with his first victory on 21 March – the day Operation *Michael,* or the *Kaiserschlacht,* began. He was probably flying a Pfalz D III (as seen here) or a D IIIa. He would eventually flame 11 balloons as part of his score of 21 victories

The heavy fog that aided German storm troops on the assault's first day also hampered aerial operations. While JG I flew 52 sorties on 21 March only two victories were achieved, as 'balloon specialists' Löwenhardt and Friedrichs both followed their orders to destroy the enemies' tethered observation posts. Mists continued to limit activity for the next two days, but on the 24th Ltn Keseling of *Jasta* 10 borrowed *Jasta* 11 Dr I 147/17 for a patrol, but was brought down by ground fire and captured.

Between the 24th and the 26th Richthofen bagged the wing's entire total of four aircraft. His combat report for his 69th victory on 26 March included the first mention of a new member of *Staffel* 11;

'With five gentlemen of *Jasta* 11 at a low altitude, I encountered, with Ltn Udet, a Sopwith single-seater at the Front. From an aeroplane's length I shot him down in flames'.

As commander of *Jasta* 37, Ernst Udet had been personally recruited for JG I by Richthofen himself. The Rittmeister undoubtedly had a *Staffelführer's* position in mind for the ebullient 21-year-old, who brought a string of 20 victories with him.

LÉCHELLE

As German troops made unprecedented gains, their air units found themselves further behind the Front. As a consequence, on 26 March the entire *Geschwader* made the difficult move forward to the abandoned airfield of No 25 Sqn RFC at Léchelle. The pilots eagerly anticipated moving into the rumoured 'luxurious' living quarters of the erstwhile inhabitants, but they were sorely disappointed. It was a 'rather neglected airfield', said Bodenschatz, and the barracks were corrugated iron Nissen Huts, which made a wretched impression on all the pilots – although they did eagerly snatch up quantities of good blankets and stoves.

The enlisted men began filling in the shell craters and the staff inspected the four useable wood and canvas tent hangars, but found only 1500 litres of fuel. *Jastas* 6,10 and 11 were situated on the southern edge of the field, and *Jasta* 4 on the north. Udet wrote;

The Fokker triplanes of *Jasta* 11 were also transferred to the airfield at Awoingt, and they flew from there in the initial days of the 'Great Battle'. A variety of fuselage bands and striped or solid-coloured tailplanes are in evidence on these Dr Is, which would have displayed the *Staffel* red on their noses, wheels and struts. In the distance at left are Albatros and Pfalz scouts of *Jasta* 4

'After two days the field was quite in order. One no longer had to come down on one exact spot in order to avoid a crash-landing. The pilots and the crews had been settled into the well-known English half-round Nissen huts. Water could not be obtained in these surroundings, and had to be procured by truck from far away. Actually, it could only be used as engine coolant. For cooking, washing and brushing one's teeth, seltzer water that we had brought along in abundant amounts had to be used. Much amusement was produced by the accounting book which was left behind in the casino. We noticed that one Australian gentleman had taken around ten whiskies and the same number of other spirits for himself during one of the last days.'

Udet went on to describe the reasons for JG I's success;

'Other *Staffeln* go up two or three times a day. Richthofen and his men fly five times a day. Others close down in bad weather – here, they fly under almost any condition. Based just a few kilometres behind the lines, and often within range of enemy artillery, we are on fully dressed standby, lounging in reclining chairs in an open field. Our aircraft, fuelled and ready to go, are right alongside. As soon as an opponent appears on the horizon, we go up – one, two or an entire *Staffel*. Immediately after the fight we land, stretch out in our reclining chairs and scour the sky with binoculars. Standing patrols are not flown.'

Furthermore, Udet said, Richthofen made certain that his unit had an excellent mess, as he felt that a pilot's nerves depended on a satisfied stomach and adequate sleep.

On 27 March these procedures paid off handsomely as the thunder of aerial combat reached a crescendo, and 13 aircraft were claimed by JG I. Many of these were low-flying British machines harassing the advancing field-grey troops below. Hemer of *Jasta* 6 started the day off with his fifth victory – a 'Bristol Fighter' which was more likely a Sopwith Dolphin, as the big twin-bay single-seater was still fairly new, and was often mistaken for a two-seater. At the same time Löwenhardt scored kill 15 when he forced a DH 4 down into the shell holes.

The triplanes of *Jasta* 6 were particularly potent against two-seaters, as Janzen contributed one, Reinhard another and a third was credited to the whole *Staffel*. *Jasta* 6 had yet another new talent in Hans Kirschstein, who achieved a double on this day. His first was obtained in a famous combat which led to a Victoria Cross (VC) for one of his opponents.

Kirschstein and other pilots from *Jasta* 6 had attacked the Armstrong-Whitworth FK 8 flown by 2Lt A A McLeod and his observer Lt A W Hammond of No 2 Sqn. The two-seater was set ablaze by Kirschstein's accurate short bursts, but McLeod still managed to bring it down in no-man's land. In spite of his own burns and wounds, the pilot dragged the unconscious Hammond away from the blazing wreck, and both men were rescued by South African soldiers. Although he won the VC, McLeod fell victim to influenza on 9 November. Udet also achieved his first victory with JG I that momentous day;

'There are five of us, the Rittmeister in the lead. Behind him are Just and Gussmann. Scholz and I bring up the rear. I fly the Fokker triplane. We skim over the pockmarked landscape at a height of about 500 metres. Above the ruins of Albert, just below the clouds, hangs an RE – a British artillery spotter. We are a bit lower than he, but apparently he hasn't

Neither the identity of the *Jasta* 11 pilot nor the date of his forced landing are known, but this scene may well have occurred during the hectic days of the Offensive. After the first catastrophic problems with the triplane wings had been remedied, there were still occasional problems, as evident here. The thin plywood wrapped around the ribs that formed the leading edge of the wings could be punctured by enemy fire, and the ensuing airflow into the wing structure could tear the fabric away from the ribs themselves. The relieved NCO pilot seen here has not been positively identified, but he bears a resemblance to Vfw Edgar Scholz. His Dr I was emblazoned with an interesting fuselage band, and no doubt the typical *Jasta* 11 red coloration (*courtesy Jörn Leckschied*)

noticed us, because he quietly continues to circle. I exchange a quick look with Scholz – he nods. I separate from the *Staffel* and race for the "Tommy".

'I take him from the front. From below, I dart for him like a shark and fire at short range. His engine is riddled like a sieve. He tilts over at once and disintegrates right after. The burning fragments fall close to Albert. In another minute, I am back with the formation and continuing on in the direction of the enemy. But the Rittmeister has noticed. He seems to have eyes everywhere. His head whips around, and he waves at me.'

After landing, Richthofen strolled up to Udet, half smiling. 'Do you always bring them down with frontal attacks, Udet?' he asked, with a hint of approval.

'I have had repeated success that way', replied Udet, as nonchalantly as he could.

'By the way, you can take charge of *Jasta* 11 starting tomorrow', said the Rittmeister over his shoulder. Udet was a bit surprised at the laconic informality of this remark, but said, 'One must get used to the fact that his approval will always come in an objective manner without the least trace of sentiment. He serves the Fatherland with every fibre of his being, and expects nothing less from all his fliers'. Richthofen shot down three British aircraft himself that day, to bring his score to 73.

Two new pilots arrived at JG I that evening, and they too had been hand-picked by Richthofen. Ltn d R Richard Wenzl had transferred into aviation from the 5. *Badisches Feldartillerie-Regt* Nr 76 in 1915, and had flown with Fl. Abt. (A) 236 and *Jasta* 31 prior to joining *Jasta* 11. Wenzl's victory score totalled just one, but this would soon increase under the

ERNST UDET

Ernst Udet was born in Frankfurt-am-Main on 26 April 1896, but soon after his birth his family moved to Munich. When war came in 1914, he managed to join a Württemberg Reserve Division as a motorcyclist-messenger. Udet then learned to fly by taking private lessons. In September 1915, he began his career as a military pilot in Fl. Abt. (A) 206. Two months later he transferred to Fl. Abt. 68 and the unit's fighter detachment, *Kampfeinsitzer Komanndo* Habsheim, which soon became *Jasta* 15.

Flying a Fokker D III, Udet achieved his first victory on 18 March 1916 when he shot down a Farman out of a group of 22 French aircraft which were raiding Mülhausen. After his third kill, he was commissioned a leutnant der reserve in January 1917, and continued to fly in *Jasta* 15 under Gontermann. It was with *Jasta* 15 that Udet reportedly had his famous fight with the French ace Guynemer in June 1917. He wrote that during the dogfight his guns jammed, and the Frenchman chivalrously broke off the combat when he saw Udet hammering on their breeches.

In June 1917 Udet transferred to *Jasta* 37, and rose to command this unit in November 1917. He brought his tally to 20 kills there, flying the Albatros D V and D Va. His various fighters were all decorated with his familiar 'LO!' emblem, which was Udet's nickname for his fiancée, Eleonore Zink.

In March 1918 he was asked to join JG I by Richthofen, and he jumped at the chance. Udet commanded *Jasta* 11 until 8 April, scoring three more victories flying the Dr I. A painful ear infection sent him to hospital, and he was at his parent's home when news of his *Pour le Mérite* arrived. When fully recovered, Udet returned to take command of *Jasta* 4 on 20 May. By late June he was flying the D VII, although he may still have used the Dr I at times. His score increased steadily, but once he received the BMW-engined D VII on 30 June his victories came rapidly. In the summer of 1918 Udet engaged in a friendly scoring competition with Erich Löwenhardt of *Jasta* 10. He survived the war with 62 confirmed kills, second only to Richthofen's 80.

After the war, Udet stayed in aviation and soon became Germany's best known pilot, a star airshow performer and a popular public figure. He travelled the world and made flying and travel films. In 1935 he was persuaded to join the new Luftwaffe, and rose to high rank. Once the war started, Udet was not temperamentally suited to the responsibilities of his post as Technical Bureau Chief of the *Reichsluftfahrtministerium,* nor was he able to deal with the political intrigues of his superiors like Göring and Erhard Milch. Depressed, desperate and addicted to drugs and alcohol, he took his own life in Berlin on 17 November 1941.

teachings of his old technical college friend Ltn d R Hans Weiss, who arrived at the same time. A native of Hof, on the Austrian border, the 25-year-old Weiss had gone through the usual two-seater experience before being transferred to *Jasta* 41, where he picked up ten victories, and Bavaria's Military Merit Cross. Weiss and his comrade Wenzl would both prove skilful exponents of the Dr I.

The deadly pace continued unabated on the 28th. Flying Dr I 149/17, Udet survived a hair-raising test of wills with Canadian Camel pilot

Ltn Ernst Udet scored his first JG I victories flying as a commander of *Jasta* 11 in March and April 1918. After a convalescent leave, he would return in late May to take over *Jasta* 4 and lead it for the remaining months of the war

Ltn Hans Weiss had scored his first victories in *Jasta* 41 before arriving at JG I. He flew briefly with *Jasta* 10, before going to *Jasta* 11, where he brought his total up to 16. Weiss flew Dr I 545/17, marked with a white upper wing, rear fuselage and tail surfaces, as well as the usual *Jasta* 11 red colouration. He was shot down and killed on 2 May 1918, and was duly buried alongside Edgar Scholz, Robert Eiserbeck and Hans Joachim Wolff

This Fokker Dr I is undoubtedly Richthofen's 127/17, seen in its red decoration. The Rittmeister is probably the figure third to the left of the triplane (marked with an 'X' on the original photo), wearing a bulky *Fliegerkombination* suit and a Heinecke parachute harness. Richthofen's combat reports for his 71st, 74th and 76th victories in late March and early April describe Dr I 127/17 as having a red upper wing, cowling, struts and tail (along with red struts and wheel covers). The same colour scheme was applied to his Dr Is 152/17, 477/17 and 161/17. While the serial number of the Dr I in this photograph is not discernible, the unique camouflage streaking pattern on the wings and the worn paint around the fuselage and rudder crosses are identical to those seen in earlier photos of 127/17. This shot was probably taken at Léchelle airfield, therefore

C R Maasdorp of No 43 Sqn, and wrote (as translated by O'Brien Browne);

'I was flying with a comrade (Gussmann) near Albert at a height of 400 metres – 500 metres above us, some Sopwith Camel single-seaters showed themselves. I yanked my triplane upwards and shot at one of the Camels almost vertically from below. He immediately attacked and began banking with me. I soon figured that my opponent was an experienced flier. He attacked me directly from the front, from the same height – in such cases both aircraft fly a hair's breadth from each other. It is a unique feeling, and it requires great calm – to aim well when you see that the opponent whom you are shooting at is himself shooting, and is increasing in size every second. You must carefully make sure that you don't ram into each other when flying by.

'As the Englishman came on for the third time, he immediately received several hits from me at an extremely close range. His aircraft turned over, and would have rammed me if I hadn't slipped over onto my left wing at the right time. The vanquished opponent dropped 100 more metres and then hit a shell crater with a crash.'

A shaken Udet returned to Léchelle, drenched with sweat and feeling a dull throbbing pain in his ear.

That same day, Weiss claimed a victory during his brief stint with *Jasta* 10, and Ltn Viktor von Pressentin *genannt* von Rautter of *Jasta* 4 also brought down a Camel to notch up the first of fifteen victories. The day's fourth success was provided by Richthofen's 74th claim (a FK 8). However, *Jasta* 4 lost its leader when Hans-Georg von der Osten was severely injured after his aircraft was sent crashing to earth near the Albert-Bray Road. Although his injuries left him with no memory of the specifics of his crash, he did recall many years later;

'I was flying a Pfalz D III, not an Albatros as is stated by Bodenschatz. Alas, it was a Pfalz, and these Pfalzes had a nasty habit of slipping in a turn. The aircraft was smashed so I don't know whether the Britisher shot my aeroplane to pieces or whether I just slipped and crashed.'

He would not return to active duty.

Ltn Johann Janzen was moved from *Jasta* 6 to take temporary command of *Jasta* 4, and he later wrote;

'The change that I made was not a good one, since *Jasta* 4 still used the old Pfalz D III, which in their aged state could only reach an altitude of about 3000 metres, where they were invariably pounced upon by a bunch of cheeky SE 5s. The *Staffel* only scored three victories in April, and I myself was unable to score any, despite intensive patrol work.'

Most of the *Geschwader's* victories in these hectic days were, in fact, achieved by the triplane pilots of *Jastas* 6 and 11. In later years, the 18-victory pilot Franz Hemer of *Jasta* 6 would write;

'The triplane was my favourite fighting machine because it had such wonderful flying qualities. I could let myself stunt – looping and rolling – and could avoid an enemy by diving with perfect safety. The triplane had to be given up because although it was very manoeuvrable, it was no longer fast enough.'

Vfw Franz Hemer of *Jasta* 6 poses with his well-worn Fokker Dr I. Unusually, the Iron Cross insignia on the underside of the bottom wing has a narrow white border. The black-painted cowling shows evidence of considerable use. A former concert cellist, Hemer was also a virtuoso in a triplane, scoring at least eight victories with the type in March-May 1918. Having brought his score to 18 flying the D VII, he was wounded on 9 August 1918. During his convalescence Hemer gained a well-earned promotion to leutnant, and returned to *Jasta* 6 in late September but apparently did no more flying. He was awarded the Knight's Cross of the Royal House Order of Hohenzollern on 8 November, one of the last such awards of the war (*N W O'Connor*)

On 1 April 1918 the Royal Air Force was officially created by combining the Royal Flying Corps and Royal Naval Air Service, but this made little difference to the German airmen, as the cloudy skies of the past several days had cleared and the contest for supremacy resumed. Hemer and his *Jasta* 6 commander Reinhard each claimed victories, with two more going to the 22-year-old Hans Joachim Wolff of *Jasta* 11. '*Wölffchen*' deeply wanted to follow in his mentor Richthofen's footsteps. He had experienced a run of bad luck up till this point, but the next weeks would see his career take off.

The Rittmeister reached a milestone on 2 April, and a journalist was there to record it. Peter Lampel left an evocative account of *Jasta* 11 during the Offensive. Richthofen began the day well by reaching the three-quarter-century mark with an RE 8. He stalked the machine at 1230 hrs and shot it down in flames from a height of only 30 metres. Shortly thereafter, as Richthofen was chatting with Lampel, a telegram arrived with the news that, 'His Majesty has conferred the Order of the Red Eagle, Third Class with Crown and Swords, on the Rittmeister. That's a regimental commander's order'. Richthofen was heartily congratulated and (according to Lampel), actually blushed.

However, there was little time for celebration as the Rittmeister was heading off to the Front in a vehicle to search for yet another new airfield. He appointed Hans Weiss to lead *Jasta* 11 on its afternoon patrol at 1600 hrs in his absence, and after a brief nap and some coffee, the Dr I pilots left;

'The take-off amazes me. I have never seen such manoeuvrability in an aircraft. A short take-off run – only a couple of metres – and then an almost vertical climb-out on the left wing, the nimble little crate practically hanging on the propeller. Wolff is the first to take off. He is in an incredible mood today, and so he does a couple of incredible aerobatics. Of course! The Rittmeister isn't there!'

After a brief interval, the red-nosed triplanes returned;

'The obligatory question: "Did you shoot anything down?" "Yes, sir! Wolff got one". "Where *is* Wolff?" "There – he's just now landing, rolling up". "Hello, Wolff! Congratulations!" His whole face is beaming. "Weiss got one too!" he says. And now a third man reports in – Vfw Scholz. From everything he says it is clear the fight is still reverberating inside him.

Jagdstaffel 11's colourful triplanes are neatly lined up in front of the Bessoneau tent hangars at Léchelle, which were left on the airfield by No 15 Sqn in early April 1918. The second Dr I from the right, marked with a swastika, was previously flown by Ltn Eberhardt Mohnicke, and is seen in the earlier line-up photographs with iron cross markings – Mohnicke had previously served in *Kagohl* 2, and he brought the swastika marking with him from that unit. When this photo was taken Mohnicke was not with the unit, having been wounded in Dr I 155/17 on 1 March. The fuselage aft of the cockpit was a pale colour such as light blue, but now the rudder has been painted white as specified, and the Balkenkreuz insignia added. In front of the aircraft are three ill-fated triplane pilots. At left is Uffz Robert Eiserbeck, who was killed on 12 April 1918, the 16-victory ace Ltn Hans Weiss, who was killed in action on 2 May 1918, and Vfw Edgar Scholz, who died in a crash on the same day as Weiss

'But Ltn Weiss says, "*Ja*, but I don't know for sure that he fell. I'm flying towards the *Staffel* and I see a bright streak in a hole in the clouds above me. As I put my crate into a turn – and you knew right away why I was making a climbing turn – all at once I see seven enemy airmen. And now we're climbing straight up into the hole in the clouds like we're in a lift. Wolff is right next to me, then Gussmann. There's five of us against seven of them. At first the "Tommies" see only me – I make yet another turn as if I intended to run away, and they just press me all the harder. There – another turn – and I'm right in the middle of them.

'"At first I shoot it out with two of them and then I single out the one and pursue him – he dives under the clouds, with me right behind him, pumping his crate full of lead. I lose sight of him. I'm thinking that nothing's come of it, and together with (Ltn) Just, I latch onto yet another two Bristol Fighters, but they haul out of there with their tails in the air".

'"Not quite", says Ltn Gussmann. "I saw the whole thing. I flew a couple of hundred metres away from you, saw you engage the Bristol Fighters, saw them both dive into the clouds. Right away I went into a spin too, and right below where he went into the clouds, I saw the Tommy pull out of the spin and break up – one of his wings broke off in mid-air".'

Just then, Gussmann related, he had a connecting rod break in the Oberursel engine of his Dr I. Despite the danger of his engine falling to pieces, Gussmann stayed in the fight to support his comrades. Then Wolff recounted his portion of the tale;

'But then all at once another one is coming at me, at least 100 metres away. I start firing at him, even if he is a bit far. I hold steady, take precise aim and then he flies right into my line of fire, burns immediately and crashes. I look around for a moment. Was there anyone else firing at him? No, honest! He's mine. So I see half the operation from down below, and I see Weiss finish off his man.'

Soon the pilots were in the officers' mess, hurriedly scribbling down the documentation for Wolff's fourth and Weiss' fourteenth victories. As they prepared for yet another sortie that evening, a group of *Jasta* 6 triplanes returned. 'Hello! We shot down *two* this time!' yelled the jubilant *Staffel* 6 pilots, referring to claims by Kirschstein and Paul Wenzel. The *Jasta* 11 pilots replied, 'That doesn't impress us at all. We got three!'

The five victories achieved on 2 April were satisfying, but Richthofen knew they were due more to the skill and daring of his pilots than the quality of their aircraft. He had already recognised the faults of the Fokker triplane, and was eager to receive the promised Fokker D VIIs. Once again, in a letter to his friend von Falkenhayn at *Kogenluft*;

'When can I count on Fokker biplanes with the super-compressed engines? The superiority of the British single-seater and reconnaissance aircraft makes it even more perceptibly unpleasant here. So please give me news soon about when we can count on new machines.'

In the meantime, Richthofen felt the *Geschwader* was already too far behind the Front. He had scouted out an advance landing field at Harbonniéres, only eight kilometres from the frontlines. In a few days the field was ready – the *Geschwader* triplanes would fly from Léchelle to the advance field each morning, sortie from there on the day's patrols, then return to Léchelle in the evenings. Eight tent hangars were pitched for the triplanes in case of rain, with British bell tents for the enlisted men.

Although accommodations were primitive, the food was still good. Richard Wenzl wrote in his book, *Richthofen Flieger* (translated by Jan Hayzlett);

'Even up there in Harbonniéres, rations were provided in a tent. Bodenschatz, the tireless one, would fly beer and food up in a DFW (two-seater), and so when we came home dead tired in the evenings, most of the time there was a princely meal there for us. A man can't fly without good rations.'

The Harbonniéres advance field was baptised with ten victories on 6 April – the first day of operations. The triplane experts reaped a grim harvest, Kirschstein and Hemer of *Jasta* 6 and Udet, Scholz and Just of *Jasta* 11 each claiming one, while Weiss and *'Wölffchen'* each claimed doubles, while the Rittmeister flamed yet another Camel for his 76th.

However, the *Geschwader* temporarily lost a valuable *Staffel* leader that day. Udet's ear troubles had been growing worse, and he had already paid a brief visit to a military hospital. When he landed after downing a Camel that morning, he had been in such intense pain he stumbled past Richthofen without acknowledgment and went to see the group's medical orderly – his inner ear was badly infected. Shortly, the Rittmeister entered the room and ordered, 'Now be gone with you, Udet'. Although the sickly *Jastaführer* protested (hating to break the momentum of his 'lucky streak'), he acceded and left on medical leave the next day, with his flying future in doubt. His place as *Jasta* 11 leader was taken by another fast-scoring newcomer, Hans Weiss.

On 7 April Richthofen once again led *Jastas* 6 and 11 in a successful ambush of 18 Camels from No 73 Sqn. One of the Camels (flown by 2Lt A Gallie) was shot to pieces by the Rittmeister, who received credit for two victims this day. Kirschstein brought down Lt Ronald Adams, who was captured, and Wolff was also credited with another fighter. It appears that No 73 Sqn lost only Gallie and Adams, however, with other Camels being shot up. Ltn Gussmann received a minor wound to his right leg.

With 12 victories achieved in two weeks, Richthofen may have felt that his glory days of 'Bloody April' a year before had returned.

Although Lothar was still in hospital, the Rittmeister had welcomed yet another relative to *Jasta* 11 – Ltn Wolfram von Richthofen, a distant

A broader view of the *Jasta* 11 triplane line-up with Dr I 127/17 at the end, and an unidentified pilot in a parachute harness at right. A stepladder stands ready to help Richthofen climb into his triplane. The other aircraft display various decorations on their fuselages and tails. Fourth from left is a Dr I marked with black(?) and white stripes on its rear fuselage, tailplane and rudder, and a light-coloured X on a dark field. This marking was similar (but not identical) to the motif which adorned the two triplanes flown by Steinhäuser, and also Dr I 502/17

cousin. Wolfram, or 'Ulf', was a 22-year-old ex-hussar who had yet to earn his first victory, but who would eventually score eight times in *Jasta* 11.

CAPPY – THE RINGMASTER FALLS

For the next few days, the focus of Germany's assault forces turned to the 4. and 6. *Armee* Fronts as the Lys Offensive was initiated on 9 April. Together with poor weather, this brought a brief respite to the units of the 2. *Armee*. On the 8th, a new airfield one kilometre south of Cappy was scouted out, and preparations began for JG I to move again. The transfer was completed by the 12th, and all personnel were now housed in 100 British bell tents, with 40 tent hangars having to suffice for the aircraft – soon British Nissen huts would be set up as more permanent barracks.

The group's pilots saw considerable action that busy day. Richard Wenzl wrote;

'Most of the time we (*Jasta* 11) were flying in two *Ketten* in order to achieve better success. Scholz, "*Wölffchen*" and Eiserbeck flew with Richthofen, while Steinhäuser, Gussmann, Just, Oblt Karjus and I flew with Weiss.'

Between 1225 hrs and 1400 hrs, four aircraft fell to pilots of *Jastas* 4, 10 and 11, for the loss of Uffz Eiserbeck, whose triplane crashed following combat. In addition, a *Jasta* 6 leutnant known as 'Wolff III' to distinguish him from namesakes Kurt and Hans Joachim was lightly wounded – he would stay with the *Jasta*, but received more serious wounds only a week later. He did not return until August.

On the 13th, all the work on the airfield and quarters at Cappy was abruptly halted – the 6. *Armee* desired the *Geschwader* for the upcoming Kemmel Offensive, and contradictory rumours had circulated as the headquarters of the 2. and 6. *Armee* groups argued over who would get JG I. As of 13 April orders were received for the move to Lomme airfield, near Lille, in the 6. *Armee* sector. Over the next two days much of the group's ground personnel travelled to Lomme and began preparing the airfield, but the aircraft and their pilots were grounded by bad weather. Then on the 15th the skies cleared and, as Wenzl wrote, 'We stood ready at our machines. Richthofen was already pulling on his sealskin boots when a rider came up and called everything off again'.

The frustrated support personnel were then ordered back to Cappy, and everybody was finally back in place by the 17th. All of this chaos must have been extremely irritating for the exhausted Rittmeister, for in spite of his rapid scoring at this period, it is evident his head wound and the duties of command had taken their toll. In a private reflection written at this time, he said;

'The battle now taking place on all Fronts has become dreadfully serious. I am in wretched spirits after every aerial combat. When I put my foot on the ground again at the airfield, I go to my four walls. I do not want to see anyone or anything.'

By the 20th, the *Geschwader* was back in action as fair weather arrived, and according to Wenzl;

'The sky was swarming with enemy single-seaters and two-seaters. Again Richthofen shot one down (he actually got two on 20 April, his 79th and 80th kills). Weiss also got his man this particular day (his 17th). This flying in two *Ketten* very much proved its worth.'

Ltn d R Justus Grassmann transferred into aviation from a field artillery regiment in the autumn of 1916. After service as a pilot in Fl. Abt. 32, he trained as a fighter pilot and reported to *Jasta* 10 in October 1917. Grassmann is seen here in a Pfalz D IIIa. He did not begin scoring until given a D VII in June 1918, but then attained ten victories. His last was scored on 6 November 1918, and during this combat he was slightly wounded. His Fokker D VII and, presumably, his Pfalz, had brown and white striped elevators and horizontal stabilisers as personal markings

Richthofen's all red Fokker Dr I 425/17 was photographed at Léchelle in late March 1918, before its crosses were altered to *Balkenkreuz* format. Other *Jasta* 11 triplanes are visible in the background. Richthofen died in this aircraft on 21 April, and many portions of its fabric survive – as well as many faked pieces! Close examination of various authentic fabric pieces by experts like A D Toelle have failed to uncover any evidence of the olive green streaked camouflage beneath the red paint, although the light blue undersurface paint is present. This, along with the immaculate finish, may suggest that this Dr I was painted red at the factory for Richthofen. Some have argued that the Dr I pictured is actually 477/17. However, all of Richthofen's combat reports (including his 78th victory of 7 April, at Léchelle) which describe 477/17 state it had only a red upper wing, rear fuselage/tail and cowling – thus it seems very likely that this is 477/17

The fateful events of 21 April 1918 have been examined, discussed and argued over in with great enthusiasm ever since they occurred. It is beyond the scope or intent of the present work to detail the controversy over 'who shot down the Red Baron'.

The day dawned with a drizzle and heavy grey ground mist, but a strong easterly wind (unusual for the Western Front) blew this away, and at 1030 hrs British aircraft were reported approaching the Front. Again, the two *Ketten* of *Jasta* 11 triplanes roared off in pursuit. Flying Dr I 425/17, the Rittmeister led his newly-arrived relative Wolfram, Karjus, Scholz and H J Wolff – the other flight was led by Weiss.

They had a brief skirmish with two RE 8s of No 3 Sqn Australian Flying Corps (AFC), during which Weiss' Dr I was hit and a rudder cable shot through, forcing him to break off and return home. Then, joined by some Albatros fighters from *Jasta* 5, the two triplane flights became embroiled in a dogfight with Camels of No 209 Sqn. Richthofen dived on the Camel flown by 2Lt Wilfred May and pursued it along the Somme River valley all the way to Vaux-sur-Somme. Uncharacteristically, he chased the scout well into Allied territory. May's flight commander, Capt A Roy Brown, made a quick dive on the pair and fired a brief burst at the red triplane.

Although Brown was officially credited with bringing Richthofen down, there is now little doubt that the Rittmeister fell to the ground fire of the many Australian troops who were shooting at the low-flying

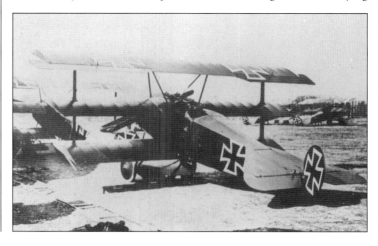

triplane. The red Dr I ploughed into a beet field along the Bray-Corbie road, and Richthofen was found dead from a single bullet through his heart. He was buried with full military honours at Bertangles the next day by an honour guard of officers from No 3 Sqn AFC.

The triplane pilots of *Jasta* 11 had returned to an airfield full of dread and uncertainty. Soon, reports came in from ground observers that the red triplane had come to earth northwest of Corbie. Despite thorough searches of the area by JG I airmen, no traces of the Dr I or its pilot were discovered. The next day Maj Haehnelt visited Cappy to inform the stunned pilots that it was now certain that Richthofen had disappeared behind enemy lines, although his fate was still uncertain (the next day a Reuters news despatch confirmed the Rittmeister's death).

Thus, on 22 April Hans Weiss led a *Jasta* 11 patrol into familiar skies over the Somme with grim determination. They were bounced by a flight of Camels from No 201 Sqn, but soon turned the tables on their attackers. Both Weiss and Richthofen's favourite Hans Joachim Wolff sent Sopwiths down, killing their pilots. Wenzl wrote of his friend and teacher;

'Weiss was leading *Jasta* 11 and did so in an exemplary manner, exactly like the Rittmeister. During these days, Weiss again shot down numerous aircraft and brought his victories to a total of 18. We shared his happiness and we liked him very much. Under his leadership, we were doing quite a bit of respectable work.'

Richthofen had left written orders that Hptm Wilhelm Reinhard, *Jasta* 6 commander, should take over leadership of the *Geschwader* if he should fail to return. These wishes were followed immediately on the 21st, and the appointment became official on the 27th. Johann Janzen was glad to leave *Jasta* 4 to return to command *Jasta* 6. Reinhard had a 'mere' 12 victories to his credit at this time, but he was a hauptmann in the regular army, and had proven himself as leader of both *Jastas* 11 and 6. He was a commander

The aircraft of the ultimate souvenir collector itself becomes a source of souvenirs. Following Richthofen's fatal flight over the Somme on 21 April, the remains of his Dr I 425/17 were brought to Poulainville. Here, members of No 3 Sqn AFC sort through the wreckage searching for pieces to take back home. The solid red tailplane and elevators are quite evident, as is a small remaining bit of the white rudder covering at extreme left. Various pieces and components of this aircraft are now held in museums and private collections in the United Kingdom, Canada, the USA and Australia

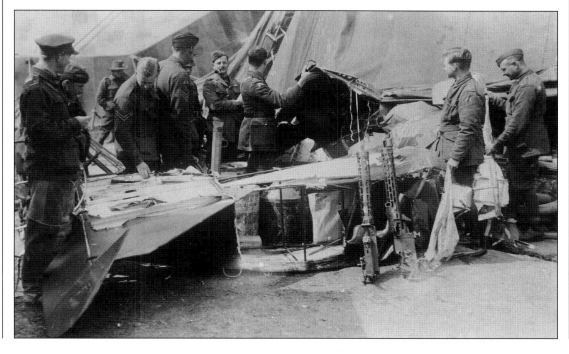

in the Richthofen mould who led by example, scoring eight more victories in seven weeks. Also like the Rittmeister, he maintained high standards for his pilots. When Vfw Willi Gabriel arrived at the *Jasta* on 19 May, Reinhard told him, 'This is no rest-camp. If you have no victories within four weeks you may remove yourself back to your (two-seater) unit'.

On 2 May 1918 a memorial service was held in Berlin, attended by the family, numerous dignitaries, and Hans Joachim Wolff and

As early as 10 March 1918, Oblt (later Hptm) Wilhelm Reinhard, leader of *Jasta* 6, had been selected by Richthofen to succeed him in the post of *Jagdgeschwader Kommandeur* if and when Richthofen failed to return. 'Willi' Reinhard was born in Dusseldorf on 12 March 1891, and had served in a Bavarian Foot Artillery regiment before transferring to aviation. He joined *Jasta* 11 on 24 June 1917, and later took command of *Jasta* 6 on 26 November. He is seen here with a *Jasta* 6 Fokker Dr I. Although Reinhard eventually scored 20 victories, and won the Knight's Cross with Swords of the Royal Hohenzollern House Order, his accidental death prevented him from receiving the *Pour le Mérite*

Wolfram von Richthofen. At the same time, Weiss led *Jasta* 11 into battle with the Camel pilots of No 209 Sqn over the Somme once again. Weiss was flying his Dr I 545/17 with its white top wing and rear fuselage when he was attacked at a range of just 20 yards by Canadian Lt M S Taylor, who shot the triplane down just south of Cerisy. Weiss' body was found with a bullet in the head and another that entered his left side through his pilot's badge. Later that afternoon 20-year-old Edgar Scholz (the six-victory NCO pilot of *Jasta* 11) stalled Dr I 591/17 when taking off from Cappy and crashed fatally. As Wenzl wrote, 'That was a lot for this one day'.

Erich Löwenhardt achieved the only victory on 2 May, but it was a notable one – he shot down the SE 5 of Maj R Balcombe-Brown, CO of No 56 Sqn RAF, who was killed.

The very next day Erich Just was wounded in the neck, taking him out of action and reducing *Staffel* 11's roster of active pilots even further. Indeed, Wenzl wrote, 'I was the only pilot of *Jasta* 11 who was fit to fly during these days. We had dwindled down that far. We flew with *Jastas* 4 or 6, and part of the time with the *Geschwader* as a unit, as well'.

The airmen of the other *Staffeln* stepped up and wreaked havoc on Allied aircraft on 3 May. Ltn Feodor Hübner of *Jasta* 4 (which now had triplanes) started the day's carnage with an FK 8 for his 2nd victory, and Aue and Friedrichs of *Jasta* 10 also claimed two-seaters. Both Ltn d R Bretschneider-Bodemer of *Jasta* 6 and Ltn Joachim von Winterfeld of

Vfw Edgar Scholz (also spelled Scholtz), the nineteen-year-old six-victory ace of *Jasta* 11, died on 2 May 1918 when his Dr I 591/17 stalled during take-off and crashed at Cappy. The Fokker's national insignia on the fuselage was painted on a white field that encircled the fuselage, but the extent of this display cannot be determined, nor can much else of this machine's markings. The message promoting Scholz to leutnant arrived just hours after the crash (*HAC/UTD*)

Ltn Friedrich Schäfer had earned the Wilhelm Ernst War Cross from Saxe-Weimar-Einsach for his work as an observer in Fl. Abt. 38. He became *Jasta* 10's Officer for Special Duty (OzbV) on 26 June 1918, having apparently previously served with the unit as a technical officer. He is seen here with a pristine Pfalz D IIIa, which has not yet been marked with the unit's yellow nose. White-bordered Iron Cross insignia adorn the underside of the lozenge fabric–covered wing, while the Pfalz in the distance displays a *Balkenkreuz* on its fuselage, dating the photo to April 1918 (*courtesy F Hallensleben via P Kilduff*)

Men of *Jasta* 10 pose together, probably sometime during the Spring Offensive of 1918 – the well-known (and often despised) Nissen huts are seen clearly. From left are Off Stv Paul Aue, Vfw Burggaller (or 'Fritz' Schumacher), Ltn Joachim Kortüm (or Nitsche), Ltn d R Julius Bender, *Staffelführer* Ltn Erich Löwenhardt, Ltn Friedrich Schäfer (perhaps the technical officer at this time), Ltn d R Hans Weiss (who scored a victory on 28 March during his brief stay in *Jasta* 10), Ltn d R Max Kühn, Vfw Aloys Heldmann and Ltn D R Justus Grassmann

Jasta 4 opened their accounts with victories, and Kirschstein and von Rautter added their own victims to bring the day's total to seven. Three more victories came to *Jastas* 6 and 10 on 4 May – the day of the double funeral for Weiss and Scholz at Cappy.

Happily, the first of the new Fokker D VIIs had finally started to arrive by this time, and *Jasta* 10 received the initial batch. On 9 May the *Geschwader* claimed four victories, followed by eleven more the next day. Richard Wenzl, still flying a Dr I with *Jasta* 11, dated the following account as 9 May, but he was apparently describing the events of the 10th;

'We took off again in *Geschwader* formation. Shortly thereafter, eight Camels fell into our clutches and there was a mad chase. In the general commotion, suddenly a Tommy came rushing past me from overhead, but his burst of fire went over me. Then he wanted to clear out. As I turned

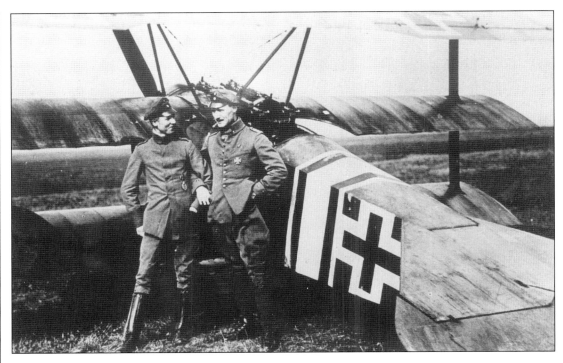

in behind him, and just as I began to fire, I was almost rammed by Reinhard, who wanted to join in. In dodging him, I had to make such demands on my machine that five spars in the upper wing broke. Reinhard vanished again just as fast as he had appeared, so I was able to get a clean shot at my Tommy until he suddenly rushed downward into the depths, apparently wounded, and made moves to land. As he did, I saw that I was being backed up by another triplane. It was Winterfeld from *Jasta* 4. Furious, knowing that there would surely be a row over the victory, I let the Tommy be and looked for another.

'The *Geschwader* reassembled because a squadron had come into view near Albert. Now a second battle began. I headed high overhead, and for the Front, in my splendid triplane. To my left, Löwenhardt in his new biplane (Fokker D VII) already had one in front of him.'

The 11 kills attained that evening included von Winterfeld's second and Löwenhardt's twentieth, putting him in line for the 'Blue Max'.

Once again there were arguments over victories. Wenzl wrote that his Camel was observed to crash by Kirschstein, but Reinhard credited it to von Winterfeld of *Jasta* 4 all the same. His differences with Reinhard caused Wenzl to ask for, and receive, a transfer to *Jasta* 6 from *Jasta* 11;

'The day-to-day quality of the *Staffeln* was changing all the time. At that time *Jasta* 6 was indisputably the best. Kirschstein became an "ace" here. The *Staffel* was in superb form, especially in the air.'

That superb form was displayed again on 15 May, as JG I airmen contributed exactly half of the 27 victories claimed by all German fighter pilots. *Jasta* 6 commander Janzen downed a DH 4 of No 57 Sqn and Kirschstein brought down three aircraft in six hours. One of these was probably the Bristol F 2B of Capt C Napier (nine victories) and Sgt P Murphy of No 48 Sqn, who were both killed, and another was a Camel

Brothers in arms – two stalwart comrades of *Jasta* 11, Ltns Werner Steinhäuser (left) and Richard Wenzl, pose for a photograph in late April at Cappy. These two were close friends and shared a barracks room, even after Wenzl transferred to *Jasta* 6 because of some disputes with Hptm Reinhard. Wenzl's Dr I in the background bore his usual black and white fuselage bands in the pattern of the Iron Cross ribbon, but with the colours reversed

Silesian nobleman Ltn Heinz *Graf von Gluszewski-Kwilicki* of *Jasta* 4 achieved his first of two victories on 15 May 1918 when he forced down this Bréguet 14B2 of *Escadrille* BR111, which landed near Harbonniéres at 1115 hrs. The crew consisted of Adj Millot (pilot) and Sgt Lavergne (gunner). Here, von Gluszewski happily cuts the swan insignia of BR111 from the fuselage – this trophy later decorated the wall of the Officers' Kasino at Bernes (*HAC/UTD*)

from the *Geschwader's* nemesis No 209 Sqn, which lost two pilots killed and another wounded in combat with JG I on this day. Two *Jasta* 4 pilots also added their first victories to the logbook, namely Sgt Otto Schmutzler and Ltn Heinz Graf von Gluszewski-Kwilicki, who was a former member of the 3. *Garde-Ulanen Regiment.* Many years later, von Gluszewski fondly recalled the Dr I that he flew at this time. 'The triplane was grand. The smoothest, lovely ship I could fly after the Pfalz and Albatros'.

16 May started off with a disturbing loss, as the popular Hans Joachim Wolff was shot down at 0820 hrs north of Lamotte Farm – only some ten kilometres from where his mentor Richthofen had crashed. *'Wölffchen's'* body was found with two bullets through his heart. Later that afternoon Ltn Hübner of *Jasta* 4 was brought down in Dr I 546/17 by the group's traditional opponents, No 209 Sqn, and captured – one of the Camel pilots involved was M S Taylor, the victor over Weiss. In addition, the *Jasta* 4 triplane of Sgt Schmutzler was shot down south of Proyart and he died of his wounds that evening.

The day's losses were troubling, but four victories were attained, as Kirschstein got a double to bring his tally to 13, and Wenzl finally broke his dry spell with an SE 5 downed at 1930 hrs.

On 17 May ten French Bréguet bombers from *Escadrille* BR20 attacked the airfield at Cappy, but *Jasta* 6 was already aloft and 'laid into them', as Wenzl wrote;

'Once again there was a real party. Kirschstein, who was a superb shot, soon sent his opponent into a spin. Under continuous fire, Janzen and I moved in behind our opponents. But a Bréguet like that dies hard – it is superbly armed. If you can picture a squadron of these bombers flying shoulder to shoulder so that an attacker is flying for the most part in a cone of fire from a whole mess of guns, then you can imagine that an attack of this sort is no small matter. Kirschstein and Janzen had also finished off their opponents.'

28-year-old Sgt Otto Schmutzler served but a brief time in *Jasta* 4. He downed a Camel on 15 May 1918 for his first victory, but died the next day, probably shot down by Lt Barton of No 24 Sqn. The off-white cowling of this Dr I was most likely a pale blue colour, as were the struts and wheel covers. These were the standard markings applied to *Jasta* 4 Dr Is (*courtesy P Kilduff*)

Though Wenzl claimed he had sent his Bréguet down 'stinking' (German pilot's slang for smoking or burning), the aircraft floated across the lines at 2000 metres and he was not credited with a victory.

The war-weary Fokker triplanes of *Staffeln* 6 and 11, with their tired Oberursel engines, were finally being phased out as more D VIIs arrived. Wenzl wrote;

'We'd had such bad experiences with our rotary engines in recent days that we were delighted to get stationary engines again. The new biplane was at least comparable to the triplane, solidarity wise. Löwenhardt, who was accustomed to getting the most from his aeroplanes, was already making all kinds of jokes about it. One of his pilots, Friedrichs, in fact, even had a spar on one of his lower wings broken by a flak shell but, nevertheless, the wing still held.'

On 18 May Wenzl received his D VII, and he had the sights and guns set up to his specifications – the next day *Jasta* 6 made its first *Staffel* patrol equipped entirely with D VIIs. Kirschstein felled yet another Bréguet, Friedrichs got a balloon and Löwenhardt and von Rautter (in a Dr I) each claimed aircraft. The successes continued the next day, with a resurgent *Jasta* 11 downing four of the five aeroplanes which JG I claimed. Two of these went to new faces, with a DH bomber being credited to Vfw Willi Gabriel, an aggressive ex-Halberstadt CL II pilot from *Schlachtstaffel* 15 who had only arrived at *Jasta* 11 that day! The second went to Oblt Erich Rüdiger von Wedel, a former Uhlan comrade of Richthofen's who had arrived at *Jasta* 11 on 23 April. He downed a SPAD for his third kill.

The *Jagdgeschwader's* last day at Cappy was 20 May. The group commemorated their departure with four victories, and welcomed Ernst Udet back to the unit to command *Jasta* 4. JG I was being transferred to the 7. *Armee* sector in preparation for the Aisne Offensive. A new era was beginning as they left the muddy field at Cappy, as from this day on they would carry a new name into battle. A telegram arrived from *Kogenluft* von Höppner, declaring that thenceforth the group would bear the name of *Jagdgeschwader Freiherr von Richthofen* Nr I.

NEW LEADERS, NEW AIRCRAFT

The German 7. *Armee* finalised preparations for the offensive on the Chemin des Dames (the Third Battle of the Aisne) in mid-May 1918. Under Reinhard's command, *Jagdgeschwader* Richthofen was moved to various airfields around Guise as the new site at Puisieux Farm was being prepared. The pilots gratefully used the next five days to rest up and acquaint themselves with their Fokker D VIIs (*Jasta* 4 still had triplanes). Secrecy was vital, and they were permitted to fly only over the rear area.

On the evening of 26 May the D VIIs and triplanes landed in the dusk at Puisieux Farm, and tent hangars were only pitched at 2200 hrs. At 0200 hrs on the morning of the 27th, 'the heaviest barrage I have ever heard suddenly commenced', wrote Richard Wenzl. 'It was indescribably glorious – the terrible shaking and vibrating of the air, the pounding and thundering in which everything was submerged. At precisely 0420 hrs, the infantry assault commenced, and as we made our way to the field, the Chemin des Dames was long since ours.'

Heavy fog hampered aerial operations on the 27th, and only Ltn von Rautter of *Jasta* 4 obtained a victory, downing a Bréguet at Pont-Arcy. The German forces made such amazing gains that by the 30th they were at Chateau-Thierry, on the Marne. That day Reinhard sent Bodenschatz

Pilots of *Jasta* 4 cavort in front of their commander Ernst Udet's Dr I at Beugneux-Cramoiselle airfield -- note the burnt French hangars in the background. After *Jasta* 6 received Fokker D VIIs, some of its triplanes were handed over to *Jasta* 4 – among them Kirschstein's Dr I 586/17, which was taken over by Udet. He flew this machine in its original markings, but with his familiar *LO* emblem added to the fuselage. These pilots are, from left to right, Ltns Julius Bender, Heinrich Maushake (six victories), Egon Koepsch (nine victories) and Karl 'Carlos' Meyer (four victories), while Heinrich Drekmann (11 victories) strikes a dramatic pose with the propeller. Note the Dr I in the background, marked with the 'off-white' cowling, struts and wheel covers that identified most *Jasta* 4 triplanes

In a candid photograph taken at Beugneux-Cramoiselle in July 1918, Udet (still in his pyjamas) relaxes with a cigarette while Heinz von Gluszewski is at right with his sunglasses. The weather was so pleasant that several *Jasta* 4 pilots chose to sleep outside on cots and enjoy the fresh air (*HAC/UTD*)

up in a two-seater to scout out a more forward location for the *Geschwader,* and they picked out a former French airfield at Beugneux-Cramaille (or Cramoiselle). While most of the hangars had been burned, there were still three intact – the charred hulks of Voisins and SPADs littered the field, but it needed only slight improvements to make it ready, and was close enough to the Front to observe French flight operations.

While artillery fire prevented the field's occupation on the 31st, the *Geschwader* still managed to reach the enemy, and they downed four Bréguets and one SPAD – the Richthofen pilots were embarking on a steady diet of 'French food' for the next seven weeks. One of the Bréguets fell to Ltn Viktor von Pressentin *genannt* von Rautter of *Jasta* 4 for his 15th victory near Soissons at 1255 hrs. However, the 22-year-old nobleman was then apparently targeted by SPAD pilot Gustave Daladier of SPA93. The French ace ended the East Prussian's career by shooting his Dr I down near Chaudun for his sixth victory.

BEUGNEUX

JG I made the move to its new base on the first day of June, with *Staffeln* 6, 10 and 11 based on the field to the east of Beugneux, and *Jasta* 4 at a farm just to the east. There was little useful equipment left intact by the French, but the pilots did locate some choice booty from the surrounding area, as Wenzl noted;

'We got quite an excellent old cognac, the likes of which I had seldom tasted. And there was also quite a number of cattle, chickens, rabbits and sheep – the *Geschwader* got itself a flock of 300 sheep. We had to provide for ourselves whatever we could. And that held true for fuel, too. We had some bad experiences with fuel, however. The French gasoline was too light, and our engines got terribly hot because they were getting the wrong mixture.'

On 2 June Wenzl flew his D VII to the aircraft depot at Valenciennes to have its Mercedes D IIIa engine switched out for a high-compression Mercedes D IIIaü.

Also on the 2nd, the French *escadrilles* made a determined effort to respond to the German advance during the afternoon, and paid dearly. Udet showed he had lost none of his old form by bringing down a Bréguet just before noon, and in the evening each of the four *Staffeln* participated

in the day's triumphs as nine SPAD fighters and two-seaters were claimed. Reinhard was the hero of the day, with three SPAD two-seaters taking his tally to 17. There must have been quite a cognac-fuelled celebration in the *Geschwader* that night, particularly as the news arrived that *Jasta* 10 commander Erich Löwenhardt (who achieved his 25th victory that evening) had been awarded the *Pour le Mérite*.

Löwenhardt had little time nor inclination to rest on his laurels, for on the 3rd he added another SPAD to the total of five French aircraft claimed by the group that day (including two by Kirschstein to bring his own score to 19). Perhaps with his own possible 'Blue Max' in mind, Reinhard shot down another SPAD XI two-seater on 4 June, and pilots from *Jastas* 4 and 11 added three more, including the first for Wolfram von Richthofen.

Jasta 4 had some interesting and unique mascots. In this photograph, taken at Beugneux-Cramoiselles circa June 1918, Ltns Julius Bender, Johannes Jessen, commander Ernst Udet and 'Carlos' Meyer are entertained by the interplay between a dog named Spad and their pet baboon, named Betty. Meyer (Carlos Meyer Baldo in his native Venezuela) recalled years later that Betty had been procured from a derelict zoo, and that once, as the pilots' belongings were all packed up ready for a move to a new aerodrome, she opened up all the luggage and made a mess of things! (*HAC/UTD*)

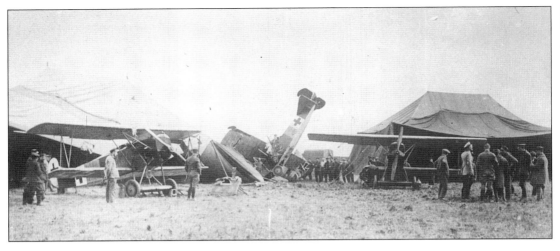

The first Fokker D VIIs to arrive at JG I went to *Jasta* 10 as replacements for the unit's weary Pfalz and Albatros. Unfortunately, Ltn 'Fritz' Friedrichs landed a bit too 'long' and ran his early D VII 234/18 into some aircraft tents and two other D VIIs. This photograph provides a glimpse of how the Iron Cross markings on these very early D VIIs were being modified to the initial thick *Balkenkreuz* insignia. They also display their 'streaked' Fokker camouflage on the fuselage sides, with light blue fuselage undersides

The Aisne Offensive was so successful that the territory gained expanded into a salient extending south toward the Marne. On 5 June the 7. *Armee Kofl* issued an order that 'air supremacy is to be secured by *Jagdgeschwadern* I and III. All captive balloons are to be shot down or forced to descend'. The seasoned 'balloon killers' of *Jasta* 10 responded, with Löwenhardt getting one and Friedrichs two. For good measure, Löwenhardt added a SPAD to the total of 11 *Geschwader* victories for the day. One of these fell to Wenzl as his fourth – he was flying as part of a joint *Jasta* 4 and 6 patrol led by Kirschstein;

'There appeared to be a lot going on northwest of Soissons when all of a sudden four Bréguets came at us and we began a lively exchange. Since our tone didn't appeal to the Bréguets, they tried to hide in a thin layer of clouds. When I dropped out of the clouds for a moment to look around, the Bréguet was right in front of me. In a flash, I was sitting just 20 metres below its tail, and pumped a burst into its fuselage. It immediately started to smoke, slowly rolled over its right wing and started to descend. It went into the ground and smashed to pieces far on the other side of the lines near Morte-Fontaine.

'At the same time, Kirschstein shot down his opponent in flames. As usual Löwenhardt, the leader of *Jasta* 10, was working as hard as he could with Udet. Friedrichs of *Jasta* 10, Reinhard, Steinhäuser, von Wedel and Bender (*Jasta* 4), and above all, Janzen were doing their best.'

JG I was, in fact, credited with 43 French aircraft and balloons from 31 May to 8 June.

The German Noyon-Montdidier Offensive opened on 9 June, and the pilots of *Jastas* 10 and 11 did their part by accounting for five SPADs and a Bréguet. However, the group suffered another significant casualty. Johann Janzen, the talented *Jasta* 6 leader, wrote;

'I had some pretty good luck with my *Staffel,* and we were able to increase our score on almost every flight at this time. My personal score rose to 13 confirmed victories. I had brought down five French machines between 25 May and 9 June, four of these being SPADs. But my luck was about to change drastically. I had orders to patrol with my *Staffel* during the early hours of the morning over the Front between Soissons and Noyon.

The 'star' of *Jasta* 6 in May and June of 1918 was undoubtedly Ltn d R Hans Kirschstein, seen here with his famous Dr I 586/17 and his groundcrew. This triplane was painted in diagonal black and white stripes on the rear fuselage and top wing in order to confuse the aim of a pursuing enemy pilot. Kirschstein also flew at least one, and probably two, Fokker D VIIs painted in a similar manner, each of which was known as '*die optische Taeuschung*', or the optical illusion, according to Richard Wenzl. Kirschstein's career as a *jagdflieger* was as brilliant as the décor of his aircraft. Between 18 March and 24 June he knocked 27 Allied aircraft from the sky, including four 'doubles' in one day and two 'hat tricks' (three in a day) (*H H Munte via N W O'Connor*)

'Suddenly, an *escadrille* of SPADs was spotted coming straight for us. After the opening shots a dogfight ensued, during which I cottoned on to a SPAD and forced him to leave the fight. I followed him down, at an altitude of only 300 metres. I got him nicely in my sights, and had just begun to fire when suddenly a deluge of oil, petrol and boiling water struck me in the face. The engine seemed to be dancing about in the nose of the aeroplane, and I immediately switched off the ignition – as the propeller slowed down, I could see that I had shot one of my own propeller blades off!'

The synchronisation gear had malfunctioned. Janzen tried to glide back to German territory but crashed within French lines and was taken prisoner. Ltn Hans Kirschstein, the 24-victory *Jasta* 6 pilot who flew a dazzling D VII decorated in diagonal black and white stripes, was a logical and wise choice for acting commander of the *Staffel*.

For the next few days, rain and heavily overcast skies, and a lack of French aerial activity, gave the weary pilots some time for much needed rest-and-recreation! Wenzl noted;

'We used this time to recover, and to make our quarters comfortable. Sometimes, there were some really wild parties with the wine we had captured, because Kirschstein had requisitioned it heavily from Chateau-Thierry. He had to bring along a lot of dishes from there as well, because he had recently caused some terrible damage to the household utensils of *Jasta* 4.'

On 12 June Reinhard claimed a SPAD XI that would bring his tally to the significant 20 mark. However, *Jasta* 11 pilot Willi Gabriel put in a competing claim for the same machine. In a highly unusual circumstance, JG I's group adjutant Oblt Bodenschatz asked Gabriel to relinquish his victory claim, thereby

Willi Gabriel strikes an intimidating pose by his Mercedes-engined Fokker D VII 286/18 before the aircraft had received the lengthwise orange stripe along the fuselage. Gabriel was an able exponent of the D VII, especially the BMW-powered version, and shot down four aircraft on 18 July, raising his tally to eleven (*A Imrie via HAC/UTD*)

Things are not always as they seem. At first glance this appears to be a rather confident British pilot – in a tight-fitting tunic – on the *Jasta* 4 airfield, but it is actually Ltn d R Heinrich Maushake, engaging in a little costume prank for the camera. Maushake, the 'well-fed *Braunschweiger*', scored six victories with *Jasta* 4. In his book *Mein Fliegerleben*, Udet refers to Maushake as *Mausezahn* or 'Mousetooth'. *Jasta* 4 triplanes are lined up in the background (*HAC/UTD*)

allowing the *Geschwader* leader Reinhard to be put forward for the *Pour le Mérite*. As a mere vizefeldwebel with four victories, Gabriel agreed to this request, as Bodenschatz promised that if such a dispute between the two occurred again Gabriel would receive the credit. As it turned out, Gabriel never had the opportunity.

On 18 June Reinhard left the *Geschwader* to attend the trials of the new fighter types at Adlershof, near Berlin. These evaluations of fighter prototypes by experienced frontline pilots had been a brainchild of Richthofen's, thus it was fitting that JG I be represented. Other JG I members who attended these trials were Ltn Hans Kirschstein (who was nonetheless back at the Front by 24 June, when he achieved his 27th victory) and *Geschwader* technical officer Fw Ltn Fritz Schubert. The diminutive and high-spirited Kirschstein was finally awarded his own overdue *Pour le Mérite* and proudly wore the order at Adlershof.

In Reinhard's absence, the question of who would take temporary command of the *Geschwader* seemed to rest between two highly qualified, and competitive *Pour le Mérite* aces – Ltn d R Ernst Udet, commander of *Jasta* 4 with 30 victories, and *Jasta* 10 leader Ltn Erich Löwenhardt with 27 at that point. On 18 June the acting command was given to Udet, but for some reason the very next day Löwenhardt was given the post. No reason was given, but Löwenhardt was a regular army officer with Prussian Cadet Corps training. At any rate, this did not seem to affect the friendship between the two, nor their deadly scoring streaks which continued unabated.

THE BMW FOKKERS

There was considerable excitement in *Jasta* 11 on 22 June, when the first shipment of 22 D VIIs equipped with the superb 'over-compressed' BMW IIIa engines of 185 hp arrived. *Jagdstaffel* 11 was the first *Staffel* to obtain a full complement of the new machines, and the leading *Kanonen* of the other units received them as well. Thus, Kirschstein of *Jasta* 6 obtained one, as Wenzl noted;

'While Kirschstein was in Berlin, I led *Staffel* 6 and was able to fly his BMW-engined aircraft, which gave me great pleasure. This machine could reach 6000 metres' altitude in 24 minutes. The effect of these new machines was seen immediately. *Staffel* 11 shot down many, for now it was easy to reach the extraordinarily high-flying French reconnaissance aircraft and shoot them down.'

The Fokker pilots continued to reap a grim harvest of French aircraft. Still flying his Mercedes D VII 244/18, Aloys Heldmann of *Jasta* 10 shot down Sgt Voisin of SPA62 in SPAD S7231 at 0945 hrs. His combat report reads;

'We attacked a French squadron at 4500 metres. My opponent attempted to escape by resorting to the ruse of diving. I followed him and forced him to land near Epaux. In landing, he broke his undercarriage. Prisoner lightly wounded. Aeroplane carried red motor cowling and blue Gallic rooster on the fuselage.'

It was also during this period that Udet and his wingman encountered a SPAD pilot of great skill, as Udet recounted in his wartime book *Kreuz wider Kokarde*;

'Over the Chemin des Dames, I dove with my friend from a great height onto two SPAD single-seaters. Each of us picked one and started to bank. My opponent had his tail surfaces painted blue and the sides of his fuselage painted in the shrillest of colours. We flew tightly around each other, and soon I could determine that our skills were evenly matched.

'After we had flown about nine or ten times after each other, and had tried unsuccessfully to get one another in the crosshairs, I got a somewhat closer look at my opponent. He was wearing a fluttering scarf and a black helmet, and was, as far as I could see, clean-shaven. He looked at me for a long time, lifted his right hand up and began to wave. Spontaneously, I waved back and this was a mutual greeting which lasted five or six full banks long. Suddenly, I had the strange feeling that there was no longer even an opponent before me, rather it seemed to me like when I had practised dogfighting with my comrades.

'Our harmonic comradeship was, however, soon destroyed by a pack of German aeroplanes. These mixed themselves into our joust. I do not know what happened to my friend in the SPAD. I last saw him, hotly pursued by five aircraft, flying southeast toward his lines.'

This Fokker-built D VII of *Jasta* 6 was retired from JG I service and handed over to Fl. Abt. (A) 298. It was then fitted with a camera on the side of the cockpit to act as a high-speed photo-reconnaissance aircraft. The *Jasta* 6 zebra stripes are still evident on the tailplane and nose, and the pilot's emblem of a swastika appeared just ahead of the fuselage cross. The rudder was a replacement from a late OAW-built D VII, thus the mis-matched cross insignia. The upper wing was also from an OAW product (*HAC/UTD*)

Even though 24 French aircraft were added to the *Geschwader* victory log between 23 and 28 June, the excellent D VIIs were not immune to defeat. Wenzl's long-time friend and barracks mate Werner Steinhäuser died on 26 June, three days before his 22nd birthday. In pursuit of his 11th victory, the former artilleryman had been shot down by a French SPAD two-seater, and his red and yellow-tailed D VII crashed to earth near Neuilly at 0800 hrs. On the day of Steinhäuser's burial – 28 June – the *Geschwader* pilots had a stellar morning's work as they accounted for nine SPADs in just over four hours, with the victories nicely distributed amongst all four *Staffeln*.

On 26 June ten-victory *Jasta* 11 ace Werner Steinhäuser was killed in combat with a French two-seater. The wreckage of his early Fokker-built D VII shows that the tailplane and elevators were decorated in red and golden yellow stripes, similar to his earlier triplanes. These were Steinhäuser's personal colours from his old unit, *Feld-Artillerie Regt* Nr 61. The underside of the streaky camouflaged fuselage was light blue. Willi Gabriel recalled seeing this D VII suddenly rear up, stall and dive away after its pilot was hit. On its way to the ground it did a series of gigantic loops, stalls and dives; Steinhäuser's body was found with a bullet in the head

Two of these were fighters of *Escadrille* SPA159 that fell to Eberhardt Mohnicke of *Jasta* 11. His first victories in over nine months (following recovery from a wound), they brought his total to nine.

The next day (29 June) saw Udet's 'greatest misfortune and greatest good fortune'. Leading a morning patrol in his well-known Mercedes-engined D VII with the striped upper wing and *Du doch nicht!!* marked on the elevators, he dived on a Bréguet flying at a height of 800 metres. He fired his first burst at a range of 80 metres, and noted that the observer had sunk from sight into the fuselage. Assuming that he was wounded or dead, Udet closed in from the flank, but was shocked to see the French observer jump up to his guns and pepper his D VII. Udet's elevator and control cables had been shot away and the Fokker plunged earthwards.

At only 400 metres, Udet unbuckled his belt and took to his parachute – a relatively new and untried device. He immediately felt a powerful jolt to his back and managed to see that 'my parachute (harness) and I were hanging on the projecting tip of the rudder'. As death seemed certain, odd thoughts ran through his mind. He recalled that he wore a brand new tunic – 'all for nothing' – and because he bore no papers or medals, his body would be unrecognisable. He thought of his fiancée and his mother, then, 'Summing up the last of my strength, I broke off the tip (of the rudder) and fell free'. Then came a violent jerk – the canopy opened at a mere 80 metres above the ground and he landed hard, spraining his left ankle;

'Everything would have gone quite nicely if I had not come down 200 metres behind our lines in the midst of a barrage – everywhere, mighty fountains of earth were heaving up. I threw away everything that was in my way and ran, as well as I could, towards the east.'

He survived a harrowing run through the bombardment and eventually made his way back to the *Geschwader*. Incredibly, that afternoon he flew another sortie.

Udet shot down a SPAD the following day for his 36th victim – apparently on his first patrol in one of two BMW-engined Fokkers he had

This unique photo was provided by Wouter Warmoes, and shows Udet's close companion, and wingman, Heinrich 'Heinz' Drekmann of *Jasta* 4, with his highly decorated D VII – thanks go to Manfred Thiemeyer for providing the identification. Udet wrote that when he managed to obtain two BMW-powered Fokkers from *Jasta* 11, he flew one and gave the other to Drekmann, and they flew many patrols together. It seems likely that this is that BMW D VII. Drekmann was born in the Hanseatic city of Hamburg, and the emblem is a cog (*Kogge*), which was the main ship used by the mercantile cities of the Hanseatic League. The author believes this D VII was probably overpainted in black (although since the Hanseatic colours were red and white, that is also possible). Black was the *Jasta* 4 colour, and would have served to differentiate Drekmann's D VII from Udet's red D VII, in the background, which was important for the confirmation of victories by observers (*photo courtesy Wouter Warmoes, information and identification courtesy M Thiemeyer*)

secured for *Jasta* 4. The same day *Jasta* 10's Friedrichs, Löwenhardt, Grassman and Schumacher flamed four balloons (two of them falling to Friedrichs) and a SPAD. However, *Jastas* 10 and 11 both lost a pilot killed.

Udet was extremely impressed with his new BMW-powered D VII's capabilities;

'I noticed more than ever its tremendous advantage over the other Mercedes-engined machines of my *Staffel*. I gave the second BMW machine to Ltn (Heinrich) Drekmann, and we carried out many patrols together. We now used to cross the lines at a height of 5900 metres, which had not been possible with other engines, and we could stay at this altitude six to twelve miles behind the enemy lines without being spotted. Our fights began mostly with surprise attacks, giving us the tactical advantage usually resulting in victory.'

ANOTHER *GESCHWADER* COMMANDER FALLS

While Udet and other pilots were making the most of their powerful new Fokkers, a tragic development took place in Berlin. On 3 July Hptm Wilhelm Reinhard flew a radical new design at the Adlershof fighter competition – the all-metal Dornier Zeppelin-Lindau D I (D.1751/18), which had a stressed-skin structure of duralumin. He had previously watched as Constantin Krefft, Hptm Schwarzenberger of *Idflieg* and one Oblt Hermann Göring, *Jasta* 27 commander, flew the D I.

The revolutionary Dornier fighter had not passed the official construction and delivery regulations, yet its testing was still permitted. After Göring landed, he handed the D I over to Reinhard. In an ironic turn of events, the top wing broke away when Reinhard was pulling out of a dive, and JG I lost its second commander in five weeks. His place would be filled by the same Oblt Göring, who would ride his fame as the last commander of the Richthofen *Geschwader* to post-war political success, and eternal infamy. One can hardly refrain from wondering how the history of the *Jagdgeschwader*, and indeed the 20th century, would have differed if the fates of Reinhard and Göring had been switched.

At the front, in the meantime, Udet continued his deadly streak by claiming two of the three victims that fell to JG I on the first day of July – one of these was a Bréguet which he downed in flames from an exhausting altitude of 6400 metres. The second day of the month, JG I encountered a new aircraft flown by a new opponent – Nieuport 28s flown by Americans.

Nine of the nimble Nieuports from the 27th Aero Squadron, in two flights, were out on patrol early that morning. Udet had been hoping he could spend the morning in bed, when his rest was disturbed by the sound of flak. He could see the AA fire from the airfield, and hurriedly pulled his 'combination' suit on over his pyjamas as he called to his mechanic, 'Behrend – ready the machine!'. Udet rushed to his Fokker and was soon airborne, while elements of *Jastas* 10 and 11 were already aloft. He wrote;

'I climbed to a height of around 400 metres, and was just wanting to ease off on the gas when I noticed several aircraft at a height of about 3000 metres. It was clear that five Germans and at least nine or ten Frenchmen (sic) were fighting a running battle. When I found myself above the dogfight, I recognised Löwenhardt, who was just then dealing with a Nieuport. A second opponent took this moment to dive down on him from behind. But in doing so he hadn't calculated that I had already wiggled in between to also get a word in, and immediately he received several shots through his engine and gas tank from me at extremely close range. He became greatly confused, immediately went down in a dive and attempted, in a rush, to fly over the river that divided the French from us. Thus I had to pursue him energetically in order to block his intentions. I shot at him only when he again tried to get behind his lines.

'During his landing, which took place about five kilometres behind our lines, my customer apparently became confused, slipped out of a bank just above the ground and made a tremendous crash-landing. I landed near him and went over to his aircraft in order to have a closer look at the construction details of the new Nieuport. I arrived at the wreckage and found that the pilot had broken his leg and had several scratches and bruises on his head, but otherwise was all right. We greeted each other with a handshake – when I spoke to him in French and he could not answer me in this language, I determined to my joy that I was dealing with an American today, and could now make the acquaintance of a member of an American squadron.'

The injured Yank introduced himself through gritted teeth as Lt Walter Wanamaker, and Udet gave him a cigarette. As the prisoner was lifted on to a stretcher, German infantrymen ran up to jubilantly tell Udet that three more Americans had been shot down (Löwenhardt was credited with two Nieuports and Friedrichs another, but the 27th lost only Lt E B Elliott killed, in addition to Wanamaker). As his injured opponent was carried off, Udet clambered over the wreckage of the Nieuport (serial Ni 6347) to gather the usual souvenirs.

There was an unusual postscript to this encounter. On 6 September 1931 Udet was in Cleveland, Ohio, performing aerobatics at the National

Its rarity and significance compensate for the poor quality of this photograph. The *Pour le Mérite* which glistens at the throat of Ltn d R Hans Kirschstein indicates that this shot was taken after his return from the aircraft trials at Berlin-Adlershof in late June/early July. The spectacular D VII was lavishly decorated on every possible surface (note the struts) with diagonal black and white striping. Even the undersides of the wings and the undercarriage axle 'sub-wing' were painted. Wenzl wrote, 'Kirschstein came back from leave and resumed his activity, fresh as ever. He shot an aeroplane down every day. He painted his machine in diagonal black and white stripes, claiming that they made it harder for the enemy to take aim. That is also why he called his crate "the optical illusion" and, in fact, he usually only got hit on the left wing' (*courtesy Bob English*)

That evening, Ltn Julius Bender of *Jasta* 4 nearly suffered the same fate as Friedrichs when the phosphorus ammunition in his D VII (F) 2063/18 ignited and set the Fokker aflame. Fortunately for Bender, his parachute worked well, and he came through with nothing worse than a sprained left foot. Bender's report helped explain the deadly problem with these incendiary cartridges. Göring temporarily banned the use of this dangerous ammunition, and additional cooling holes were soon cut into the cowlings of the D VIIs.

The German offensive, which had stalled at Chateau-Thierry, ended on the 17th, but *Staffeln* 4 and 6 (under the acting command of Ltn Paul Wenzel) were still credited with five Bréguets that day. Gen Ferdinand Foch launched a massive counter-offensive (the Aisne-Marne Operation) against the salient on 18 July. JG I did its utmost to stem the Allied tide, racking up 13 victories for the loss of two pilots – including the six-victory *Jasta* 10 veteran Bretschneider-Bodemer, who was shot down by Bréguet gunners. Göring scored his sole victory in JG I, claiming a SPAD in his red-nosed, yellow-tailed D VII (F) 294/18.

The impulsive Willi Gabriel scored an impressive four victories on two patrols in his BMW Fokker, but his flagrant defiance of Göring's commands would result in his eventual posting to *Armee Flug Park* II as a test pilot for the duration. Richard Wenzl of *Jasta* 6 was also involved with his Mercedes-engined D VII, and related his own version of the day's action;

'We cut off a French bombing squadron that was approaching Neuilly, intending to bomb Fére en Tardenois. I cut one of them out and really went to work on him. At first the observer was still firing, but then he was quiet. He'd had enough. My opponent crossed the lines, "stinking" and smoking, with his engine shot to pieces because I was convinced he was done for, I broke off and watched the outcome of the operation. One of my comrades (Gabriel) suddenly thought that he should intervene, and pumped another series of rounds into the Bréguet, which didn't even move but continued quietly on. It went into the ground near Igny and burned.

At some point, Willi Gabriel's D VII 286/18 came to a sad end, as it rolled into a fence and did a *Kopfstand*. This view reveals the chevron-style orange and sky blue stripes on the tailplane, and the final form of crosses on the five-colour fabric-covered wings. Gabriel recalled that the pilots of *Jasta* 11 each had two D VIIs, and he probably simply switched to his BMW-powered example (*A Imrie via HAC/UTD*)

When we got back, I got involved rather undiplomatically in throwing the dice for it – and lost my victory, naturally.'

RETREAT

These successes did nothing to slow the ground advances made by Foch's counter-offensive, which the pilots of JG I viewed with alarm – literally. By the afternoon of the 18th, they could see French observation balloons from their field at Beugneux, and by evening French shells were falling on the same field – they now began the bitter process of retreat which would be their lot for the rest of the war. That night most of the personnel moved to Monthussart Farm, northeast of Braisne on the Vesle River.

On the morning of the 19th the pilots flew their aircraft to the new field. That morning a familiar face was welcomed back to the *Geschwader* – Lothar von Richthofen arrived out of the rainy skies in the rear cockpit of a two-seater. Although his doctors had declared he was 'unfit for active service', he had managed to cajole and argue his way back to command

The newly returned *Jasta* 11 commander Lothar von Richthofen puts on his flight jacket while his father, Maj Albrecht Freiherr von Richthofen, looks on at right. Lothar was preparing to fly the *Jasta* 10 Fokker D VII 244/18 in the background, which was the usual aircraft of Aloys Heldmann, and which bore his markings of a black/white chequerboard on the tailplane

LOTHAR VON RICHTHOFEN

The 'Red Baron's' younger brother was born on 27 September 1894 in Breslau. Like Manfred, Lothar Freiherr von Richthofen joined the cavalry before the war, and went off to Belgium in 1914 with the *Dragoner-Regiment 'von Bredow'* Nr 4. This unit spent only a brief time on the Western Front before being sent off to Russia for the winter. Like his brother, Lothar was frustrated with the cavalry, and at Manfred's suggestion he began observer training in the summer of 1916. He flew missions with *Kasta* 23 of *Kagohl* 4 on the Verdun and Somme fronts, before his training as a pilot.

Lothar was then posted directly to *Jasta* 11 – an unusual transfer no doubt due to his brother's influence and 'pull'. As he had been taught by Boelcke, so Manfred tutored his brother in the skills of air combat, and on 28 March Lothar attained his first victory. He learned fast, scoring 15 more triumphs in 'Bloody April' and continuing his victory string in the next month. On the rainy evening of 7 May, *Jasta* 11 became embroiled in a swirling and confused series of combats with No 56 Sqn. Following the melee, the famous British ace Capt Albert Ball was dead, and Lothar was given credit for downing him (most modern historians, however, generally agree that Ball died due to a crash following engine failure). Six days later – the unlucky 13th – Lothar was hit in the left hip by ground fire after his 24th victory. He received the *Pour le Mérite* the next day, but this was scant consolation, as he spent five months in hospital.

He finally returned in late September 1917, to command *Jasta* 11. After an extended leave in January 1918, he returned to the Front in February and gained three victories flying the Fokker triplane in March. However, the misfortune of the 13th again paid him an unwelcome visit as he crashed his Dr I 454/17 and received severe jaw and facial injuries. This time he was out of action for four months, and thus was not at the Front when Manfred died, which severely distressed him. On 19 July Lothar returned to lead *Jasta* 11 once again for his last tour of duty. Now flying the new Fokker D VII, he soon formed a close flying partnership with Löwenhardt. 'We had a splendid understanding of each other in the air. I was happy to have found someone again, since Manfred, on whom I could rely'. Lothar brought his score to 40 before being wounded one last time on the 13th, this time in August.

After the war he married the Countess Doris von Keyserling. They had a daughter, but the couple eventually divorced. Lothar joined the *Deutsche Luft Reederei* as a commercial pilot, but on 4 July 1922 the engine of his converted LVG C VI aircraft failed and he crashed fatally.

Jasta 11 before this became general knowledge. And although his injured eye was 'still bothering me quite a bit', he made his first flight in a Fokker D VII that very day on a frontline patrol over unfamiliar territory. It was a borrowed machine which did not have the controls arranged for him, and, 'After a dogfight in which I could neither cope with my machine nor knew where I was, I was glad when, by sheer luck, I landed back at our airfield. I'd scarcely been able to discern friend from foe'. Lothar doggedly continued to fly, however, and his eyesight improved.

Lothar von Richthofen returned to the Front for the last time on 19 July 1918. Although he was still experiencing difficulties with his vision, he began flying immediately, and had raised his score from 30 to 40 by 13 August – the fateful day on which he was shot down for the third time

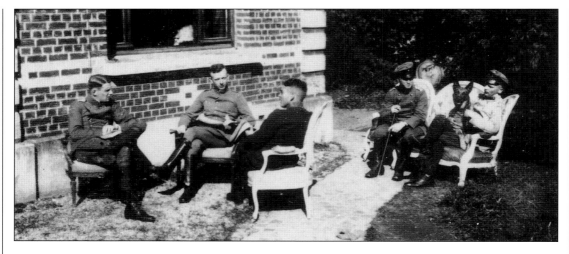

Five pilots of JG I enjoy a rare moment of leisure soaking up some summer sun outside their quarters at Braisne (Monthussart Farm) in late July 1918. They are, from left to right, Ltn Gisbert-Wilhelm Groos of *Jasta* 11, Ltn Bender and Ltn Meyer from *Jasta* 4 and little-known *Jasta* 4 pilot Ltn d R Adolf Hildebrandt, who would score his only victory on 3 November 1918. Enjoying the mascot at far right is Ltn Wolfram von Richthofen of *Jasta* 11, who was known as 'Richthofen III' in the *Geschwader.* He would reach a tally of eight kills by war's end and rise to the rank of Generalfeldmarschall in World War 2

Flying from Monthussart Farm, JG I claimed 12 aircraft and balloons from 19 to 24 July, and also strafed enemy troops, tanks and batteries. Lothar was happy to be leading *Jasta* 11 again, although aside from von Wedel and Erich Just, there were now few experienced pilots in the decimated unit. By the 25th, JG I stood at the brink of an impressive milestone, as Lothar wrote (translated by Jan Hayzlett);

'A few days later I was told, "Today's the day for the 500th victory of *Jagdgeschwader* Richthofen". The *Geschwader Kommandeur* (Göring) thought he was entitled to it, but since he was going on leave the next day, he didn't fly with us.'

Leading a group of inexperienced *Jasta* 11 pilots, Richthofen picked out a Sopwith Camel from a group of three No 73 Sqn aircraft flying above him and sent it down out of control, pumping his entire ammunition load into it for his 30th victory – and the group's 500th. He was soon lost and separated from his *Staffel*, and barely made it back after being attacked twice by RAF fighters. Upon his return, Richthofen was distressed to learn that three of his patrol were still missing. Two of them eventually turned up, but Ltn Friedrich-Franz von Hohenau had been shot down by a Camel of No 73 Sqn, and died of his injuries the next day.

On 26 July, in the midst of the bitter Allied counter-offensive, Göring inexplicably chose to go on leave, and Lothar von Richthofen was given acting command of JG I while Oblt von Wedel took over *Jasta* 11. As the German forces in the Marne salient continued to lose ground, JG I was

This less familiar aspect of Heldmann's Fokker D VII 244/18 (with Lothar von Richthofen in the cockpit) shows the black and white chequerboard tailplane. Heldmann later flew BMW-powered D VII (F) 4264/18, which was described as having a yellow nose, blue squares on the elevators (i.e. another chequered tail) and a blue fuselage

Taken from within a hangar at Braisne/Monthussart Farm at the end of July, this photograph shows one of Udet's red Fokkers at the right bearing his famous *LO!* emblem. The other OAW-built D VIIs display the black nose and wheels of *Jasta* 4 D VIIs

again forced to retreat – this time back to Puisieux Farm on 30 July. That day Löwenhardt's steady run of victories stretched to 48 with two Sopwiths, and Udet's friend 'Heinz' Drekmann of *Jasta* 4 was credited with a SPAD for his 11th victory. It was his last, however, as Drekmann was killed in the same fight, probably by SPA75 pilots.

The airmen of JG I had their last great day in the Marne Salient on 1 August 1918. Just after 0900 hrs that morning, five Nieuport 28s of the 27th Aero Squadron were sent crashing to earth by a combined patrol of *Staffeln* 4 and 6, and another fell to *Jasta* 17, all in the space of just 30 minutes. Udet, Koepsch and Jessen of *Jasta* 4 all claimed victims, as did Franz Hemer and Wenzl of *Jasta* 6, as the latter reported;

'We were flying straight for the Front when seven American Nieuports appeared from behind the clouds. Straight away, there was a great dogfight. When I looked around, I became aware that Rolff (Ltn d R Emil Rolff of *Jasta* 6) was in the middle of a real contest with an American. As Rolff later told me, this match had been going on for quite some time. The American climbed over Rolff with the help of his rotary engine, which has the advantage at low altitude, and then he attacked me too. But I couldn't allow this to happen, so I banked under him. Although he put up a desperate fight, I set him ablaze with my guns at an altitude of 1500 metres. He fell in the forest north of Fére and burned to nothing. The Americans had paid a bloody price this day. During this same fight, Hemer had finished off two opponents (one confirmed).'

Later in the day Udet claimed a Bréguet and a SPAD for his first 'hat trick'. He had used his BMW-powered Fokker to climb to 6000 metres and engage the Bréguet at a range of 90 metres – it went down and hit the ground at Muret et Crouettes, bursting into flames. Lothar downed two SPADs and *Jasta* 11's Groos got another for his seventh victory. JG I claimed eleven aircraft in total, but again not without losses. Ltn d R Walter Lehmann of *Jasta* 10 was taken prisoner, possibly by Sous-Lt Coadou of SPA88, who brought down Fokker D VII 252/18 at Villemoyenne, while acting *Jasta* 6 commander Paul Wenzel was wounded in the right arm, although he remained with his *Staffel.*

The veterans of JG I had shown that they could still inflict telling losses on the enemy, but they knew that the ground war was going from bad to worse. The drive on Paris had failed, and the Allies had now regained the initiative, and they would never lose it.

FIGHTING RETREAT

As the experienced pilots of JG I faced an uncertain future, they worried about the great number of new faces in the *Geschwader*. More uncertainty concerned another revolutionary new Fokker fighter design, the E V.

'On 5 August', noted Wenzl, 'we (*Jasta* 6) received a new aeroplane type, the Fokker "Parasol" – a monoplane with a 110-hp Oberursel-le Rhone rotary engine. Aeronautically, the machine was outstanding. We couldn't fly the machines to Laon because the troops were still unfamiliar with the Parasol, and on our first attempts to take them to the Front, we had drawn flak and ground machine-gun fire from our own side. Even our own reconnaissance aircraft had greeted us with machine-gun fire.'

Plans were already underway to return to the 2. *Armee* to set up winter quarters at Péronne. Once again the Allies altered the schedule, for in the early morning hours of 8 August, the Battle of Amiens commenced when 2000 guns of the Fourth British Army unleashed an immense torrent of shells along a 20-mile front. British infantry and tanks, supported by the French First Army, took the Germans completely by surprise. Ludendorff would later call 8 August the 'Black Day' of the German Army, but the German *Jastas* had a field day, racking up 60 victories.

Besides the famous aces Kurt Wolff and Hans Joachim Wolff, there was a third Wolff in JG I. Unfortunately, his first name is lost to history, but this Ltn d R Wolff of *Jasta* 6 was generally known as 'Wolff III' within the *Geschwader*. Here, he is seen with Fokker E V 157/18, which has been decked out with the spectacular 'petal' marking of the unit on its cowling. The pilot's personal marking was a black and white quartering on the fuselage aft of the cockpit (*N W O'Connor*)

ERICH LÖWENHARDT

The third-highest scoring German ace of World War 1 was born in Breslau on 7 April 1897. After the outbreak of war he had served in the *Kulmer-Infanterie Regiment* Nr 141, and was commissioned a leutnant before he was seriously wounded in Russia at the end of October 1914. In early January 1915 Löwenhardt returned to his unit, and served with distinction in a ski troop in the Carpathians, saving the lives of five wounded comrades. He was then transferred to the *Alpenkorps* and saw further action in the Dolomites.

Löwenhardt then requested a transfer to aviation in October 1915, serving as an observer on the Western Front. After pilot training he was posted to Fl. Abt. (A) 265 in 1916, and later went to *Jasta* 10 in March 1917. His first victory was a balloon flamed on 24 March 1917, and nine of his initial victories would be balloons. *Jasta* 10 pilot Friedrich Rüdenberg wrote that 'Löwenhardt had the right cold-bloodedness for this job'. His first was succeeded by a long dry spell, his second coming on 14 August. On 20 September he was lightly wounded, but made a smooth emergency landing near Roulers, and destroyed a balloon the very next day. Another emergency landing followed on 6 November when a wing broke – the aircraft was demolished but Löwenhardt was unscathed. By the end of 1918 he had eight kills, and was appointed

commander of *Jasta* 10 on 1 April – a week before he turned 21. Seven kills in May brought his tally to 24, and he received the 'Hohenzollern' on the 11th of that month and the 'Blue Max' on the last day.

When *Jasta* 10 acquired the Fokker D VII in May Löwenhardt's scoring rate began to increase, and once he obtained the BMW version things really heated up.

He is said to have engaged in a friendly competition with Ernst Udet in the summer of 1918, and the two ravaged both French and British aerial forces for two months. Eight aircraft fell to him in June, and 16 more in July. He could also display single-minded ruthlessness, as on 30 June when he flew with Gabriel of *Jasta* 11 on a two-man patrol. Löwenhardt dived on a British fighter and forced it to land behind German lines. He saw the pilot fumbling in the cockpit, trying to set the machine on fire. Löwenhardt repeatedly dived on the machine and drove the pilot away, who kept returning to his aircraft. The German finally killed the RAF airman with a short burst. He then landed, took the dead man's wallet and returned to the airfield. He later showed Gabriel the wallet, saying 'This is proof!'

Löwenhardt brought his prodigious score to 54 on 10 August, when his yellow D VII collided with the Fokker of Alfred Wentz. He took to his parachute, but it failed to open and he fell to his death.

Oblt Erich Löwenhardt commanded *Jasta* 10 for much of the summer of 1918, and brought his personal tally to 54 confirmed kills in an amazing string of successes – seven in May, eight in June, 16 in July (flying the BMW D VII) and six more in August, before his accidental death. Nine of his early victories were balloons

other in a hollow', wrote Lothar. He led a full *Geschwader* formation into battle that day and claimed a DH bomber for his 38th success. However, three more casualties resulted from an epic and wide-ranging scrap with their old foes – No 209 Sqn. Richard Wenzl and his namesake Paul Wenzel were among the *Jasta* 6 pilots who were shepherding the novice Ltn Bodo von der Wense along in the formation. Wenzl noted that they were far too low to deal with a large group of British bombers, escorted by the No 209 Sqn Camels, but then;

'To my dismay, Wense paid absolutely no attention and simply flew straight for the Englishmen, and away from us. By the time he realised his mistake, they were all over him. The "pennant man" was right on his tail and shot him down as I tried to intervene. Then there was a hot battle as all the single-seaters came down at us, The British "pennant man" came down and fired at me – I can still see his big red engine cowling, his broad, red insignia and his two wide red pennants on his wing struts. So we banked and turned, both of us thinking to make use of the other's weak spot. But this chap's flying was absolutely brilliant – I had never seen anything like it.

'While he was going around with me, he was firing right and left at my comrades whenever they were in a favourable position for him. But I got him right in my sights and fired with such fervour and for so long that my machine stood right straight up and lost all of its speed. As my aeroplane slowly sideslipped over its wings, he pumped my whole crate full of lead. All at once, there was a warm sensation in my hip. So I had just taken a hit. I worked my way back home and put my machine down. It was a total loss – engine, spars, radiator, everything was ruined. We counted 58 bullet holes.'

Wenzl's wound was slight, and he stayed at the Front. The 'pennant man' was almost certainly Capt John K Summers MC, who probably shot down Wense for his eighth victory and then tangled with Wenzl. *Jasta* 11 also lost Ltn d R Max Festler in this fight, probably shot down by No 209 Sqn ace Lt K M Walker for his fifth kill. *Jasta* 6's acting commander Paul Wenzel was wounded for the second time in 11 days, this time severely enough to remove him from active service for the duration.

Ironically, the *Geschwader* unknowingly exacted its revenge on No 209 Sqn very precisely the following day. Richthofen led a *Jasta* 11 *Kette* consisting of Mohnicke, Erich Just and his distant cousin 'Ulf' (Wolfram), now a seasoned veteran with three victories.

In a sky crowded with British aircraft, they were attacked by Camels from No 209 Sqn. Lothar fastened onto a fighter which was pursuing one of his men and shot it into a blazing mass with a mere 20 rounds – this was apparently the ace Lt K M Walker. Richthofen was then set upon by Capt Summers, who 'flew with exceptional skill'. Nonetheless, the German forced him down into a cratered field, where he was captured. He had become Lothar's 40th, and final, victim – half his brother's total.

Both Just and Wolfram achieved Camel victories as well, No 209 Sqn also losing novice Lt D K Leed killed in the encounter. Capt Summers was brought to Bernes and entertained by the *Geschwader* pilots, sharing a 'pleasant cup of tea' in the afternoon and wine in the evening.

The next day held ominous overtones for Lothar, who noted;

'Upon awakening in the morning, I immediately realised, "Today is the 13th – your unlucky day. The day on

The flak optical instruments used to locate and plot enemy aircraft are set up for use at Bernes airfield in August 1918. At the extreme left, with his hand on the table, is the six-victory pilot Heinrich Maushake, who would take acting command of *Jasta* 4 after Koepsch left for *Jasta* 11 in late 1918. Fourth from left, in the light tunic, is Eberhardt Mohnicke of *Jasta* 11. He survived the war with nine victories, most of which were scored in the summer of 1917. Mohnicke would be acting commander of *Jasta* 11 on three occasions (*HAC/UTD*)

Ernst Udet was at the top of his form in August and September 1918, attaining his final 22 victories. He is seen here on Bernes airfield in August 1918, with *Jasta* 4 D VIIs in the distance (see *Osprey Aircraft of the Aces 53 - Fokker D VII Aces of World War 1 part 1* page 26 for another view). At right is one of Udet's best pilots, Ltn d R Egon Koepsch, who had joined *Jasta* 4 in October 1917. He would achieve nine victories and serve as acting commander of *Jasta* 4 following Udet's departure on recuperative leave after being slightly wounded following his final victories on 26 September

which you've been wounded twice already". One mustn't be superstitious. I now intended to fly just to dispel my misgivings. On a different day, perhaps I wouldn't have taken off, for I had three different, urgent auto trips to take care of. But no – today the spell of the 13th had to be broken.'

The spell of the 13th would stay intact, however. While leading a *Jasta* 11 patrol, Richthofen was bounced by six Camels of the US 148th Aero Squadron as he was attacking a two-seater. Soon, only one man was behind him, firing at the doubtful range of 600 metres. Lothar suddenly felt an intense pain in his right leg – 'I'd taken the usual bullet', which he later claimed was the only hit in the entire machine. The Fokker plunged several thousand metres as Lothar struggled to regain both control and consciousness. Taking his right leg in both hands and lifting it onto the rudder bar, he somehow managed a landing in the battered terrain of the old Somme battlefield, weak from loss of blood. His war was over.

With Lothar back in hospital, and Göring still on his ill-timed leave, the mantle of acting *Geschwader* leader passed to Ernst Udet. One of the few old hands left, he was now the supreme living ace of the entire *Luftstreitkräfte*. He could not rest on his laurels – the war-diary for 13 August 1918 recorded bluntly, 'Due to the heavy losses of the last few days, *Geschwader* is condensed to one *Staffel*. Collaboration with *Jagdgeschwader* III and *Jagdgruppe* Greim'.

The famed Richthofen *Geschwader* had been reduced to the strength of a single *Jasta*, and this situation would be repeated several times in the upcoming weeks. The burden of attacking the enemy fell on the shoulders of Udet and a handful of old-timers. Fortunately, the unit still had enough prestige and 'pull' to transfer in some significant talent, and Ltn Arthur Laumann (commander of *Jasta* 66 with 23 victories) was brought in to take over *Jasta* 10 on the 14th.

Udet flew his red D VII (F) 4253/18 constantly, and scored daily from 14 to 16 August. On the 16th he passed Löwenhardt's total as he brought his own score to 56.

After the death of Löwenhardt, Ltn d R Arthur Laumann was brought in from *Jasta* 66 to take over leadership of *Jasta* 10. He already had 23 victories, and would increase this tally to 28 with *Jasta* 10. His Fokker D VII has some interesting cooling apertures cut into the cowling around the propeller hub

Ground personnel from *Jasta* 6 manhandle a Fokker E V into position, presumably for take-off. This view emphasises the racy lines of the monoplane, but it never lived up to its promising appearance due to engine problems and structural failures

Nine Fokker E V monoplanes and four D VIIs are seen lined up in all their glory at Bernes in August 1918. Closest to the camera is E V 153/18, flown by Richard Wenzl and bearing his usual fuselage marking. The second machine, marked with an arrow, is E V 154/18. These beautiful aircraft were only in service a short time, and only one confirmed victory is known to have been attained in them

MORE FOKKER FAILURES

One of the few bright spots in the outlook of the *Geschwader* was the promise of the sleek new Fokker E V monoplanes which *Jasta* 6 was finally taking into action from Bernes, having retrieved them from storage at Chambry. On 16 August Ltn d R Emil Rolff of the *Staffel* achieved the very first victory in an E V when he shot down a Camel of No 203 Sqn.

However, the monoplanes' rotary engines suffered from the *ersatz* oil then in use, and *Jasta* 6 pilots endured 30 emergency landings in ten days. On 19 August *Staffel* 6 engaged Sopwiths again, and Wenzl wrote that his E V 'performed splendidly' as he was working over a Camel. Then there was a sudden crack as one of his pistons failed, and the engine seized – he got it down safely but the 'Tommy' got away. When he was picked up to return to Bernes, he was shocked to hear that Rolff had crashed fatally from 300 metres as he had taken off that morning. The E V's wing had broken apart in the air and the fighter fell near the Bernes sugar factory. *Idflieg* grounded the E V immediately, pending an investigation.

Inspections showed that, as with the Dr I failures of before, sloppy workmanship and faulty assembly of the wings at the Fokker factory at Perzina was partially to blame. Condensation moisture had entered the

wings and rotted the interior surfaces. Once again new wings with varnished interiors and strengthened spars was ordered, along with tighter assembly standards, and the type (designated D VIII) was first accepted in October but never fired its guns in anger. *Jasta* 6 was given OAW-built Fokker biplanes again.

JG I still showed some of its old form on 22 August, when five British fighters fell to Laumann and Kohlbach of *Jasta* 10 and acting *Geschwader* commander Udet – Laumann and Udet got doubles. The latter brought his tally to an astounding 60, but his last victory of the day was a harrowing one, and an epic contest between two high-scoring aces.

After the debacle of the Fokker E Vs, *Jasta* 6 went back to flying the Fokker D VII – the unit received a batch of OAW-built aircraft, which were soon decorated in the unit's colours. Ltn Werner Nödecke sits on top of his D VII (OAW). The serial is obscured by the pilot's two-colour band, but it was repainted on the forward fuselage, and seems to have been either 4552 or 4532/18. This D VII was covered in four-colour fabric. Nödecke had one victory, which took the form of a SPAD downed on 3 July 1918 (*HAC/UTD*)

At about noon on 'the hottest day of the year', Udet had taken an urgent telephone call reporting RAF attacks on balloons near Brie. He took off with *Jasta* 4 and attempted to interpose his pilots between five higher SE 5s and the German balloon line. Suddenly, he saw the leading SE 5 dive right past him and head for the balloons – this was Capt Tom Hazell DSO, DFC, 'A' flight leader of No 24 Sqn, who then had 34 victories to his credit (a year before, Hazell had downed Alfred Hübener of *Jasta* 4). Udet wrote;

'I push down and go after him. It is their leader. The narrow streamer flaps in front of me. The air screams at the windshield. I must catch him, and stop him from getting to the balloons.

'Too late! The shadow of his aircraft flits across the taut skin of the balloon like a fish through shallow water. A small blue flame licks out and slowly creeps across its back. At the next moment a fountain of fire shoots up.

'In a very tight turn, the Englishman goes almost straight down. The troops at the balloon cable winch scatter, but the SE 5 has already flattened out and sweeps westward, hugging the ground – now a wild chase begins, three metres above the ground. We hop telegraph poles and dodge trees. A mighty jump – the church steeple of Marécourt – but I hang on to him.

A *Jasta* 6 pilot thought to be Hans Reimers poses in the cockpit of Fokker E V 152/18 – Gefr Kurt Blümener was also photographed in this machine. This view emphasises the streaky quality of the dark camouflage applied to the plywood-covered upper wing (*HAC/UTD*)

Udet chats on the telephone at the left inside this *Jasta* 4 hangar at Bernes. At right, his OAW-built D VII, marked with black and white borders on the lozenge-fabric fuselage, can just be seen. His customary white chevron leader's marking is seen on the tailplane and elevators (*F Hallensleben via P Kilduff*)

There is little doubt that this is Udet's D VII (F) 4253/18 of *Jasta* 4, marked with a red fuselage and tail, and of course his ubiquitous *LO!* insignia, in honour of his fiancée Eleonore Zink. This photo was taken by Rudolf Stark at Epinoy airfield on 21 August 1918. Later that day, Udet would gain his 57th and 58th victories in this aircraft (*A Imrie via HAC/UTD, information courtesy Manfred Thiemeyer*)

'The main highway to Arras. Flanked by high trees, it winds through the landscape like a green wall. He flies to the right of the trees, I to the left. Every time there is a gap in the trees I fire. Alongside the road, on a meadow, German infantry is encamped. Although I am on his neck, he fires at them. This is his undoing.

'At that moment I jump the tree-tops – hardly ten metres separate us – and I fire. A tremor runs through his machine – it wavers, tumbles into a spin and disappears in a mighty hop behind a small birch grove. A dust cloud rises.'

Despite Udet's impression, his 60th victory had not crashed, but barely made it back to Bertangles with his shot-up SE 5. Both Udet and his engine were running hot (1600 rpm), but the German ace had other things to worry about;

'I look around to see three SE 5s. They have shaken off my *Staffel* and are diving on me. I take short, quick looks over my shoulder. They are splitting up, leaving me to one of them. I know now I am dealing with proven opponents. Old fighter pilots know that in a chase you only get in each other's way. Things are looking bad for me. The other works himself in toward me – barely 30 metres – but still he does not fire. I feel a light, dull blow at my knee. I look down and notice the sweet, faint odour of phosphorus and a hole in the ammunition case. The heat – the phosphorus ammunition has ignited itself. In a situation like this, one doesn't think. One acts or dies. A squeeze on the trigger, and from both barrels the ammunition stabs out into the blue sky, trailing white smoke.'

Udet glanced behind and was astonished to see the SE 5 pulling away – he believed the pilot had been scared off by the guns' vapour trails, thinking they were tracers. At any rate, two exhausted and relieved fighter

pilots returned to their airfields that simmering August day. Both would survive the war and score again. When Udet landed at Bernes, he was so drained that he had to be helped out of his cockpit by his mechanic, Walter Behrend. He scarcely heard it when he was informed that Göring was returning that evening, and Udet himself soon left on his own leave. Koepsch took acting command of *Jasta* 4.

Udet's leadership, however, would be missed. From 23 August until Udet's return to combat on 26 September, the *Geschwader* attained 22 victories for the loss of two pilots wounded and three more killed. A respectable record, but it was a far cry from the glory days of old – even as recently as June 1918 the *Geschwader* had tallied 85 claims.

The JG I pilots were often involved in attempting to help slow the Allied advance on the ground, and on 27 August they attacked infantry and artillery positions near Foucaucourt with 'good results'. Two days later the Battle of Noyon opened, and JG I extended its patrolling area to cover the sector of the 18. *Armee* around Noyon. At the same time, the first stages of yet another move were being made, to Busigny-Escaufort. By 30 August, the move was complete, and *Jastas* 4 and 10 were settling

Udet's 60th victory was one of his hardest. This is SE 5a B8422 of No 24 Sqn ace Capt Tom Falcon Hazell being dismantled after his harrowing encounter with Udet on 22 August. Although Hazell survived and returned to his field at Bertangles, his aircraft was shot to pieces. A No 24 Sqn report says 'Capt Hazell was then seen home by the enemy aircraft, who shot his tank, longerons and propeller to pieces'. The SE 5a was sent back to an aircraft depot and was struck off strength as unrepairable

A smiling Gefr Kurt Blümener of *Jasta* 6 is prepared for flight, possibly in Fokker E V 157/18 behind him. The black and white fuselage emblem is clearly seen. The mechanic at left adjusts Blümener's Heinecke parachute harness. Ironically, Blümener jumped from his D VII during aerial combat on 8 September, but for some reason the parachute failed and he plunged to his death (*HAC/UTD*)

down northwest of Escaufort, with *Jastas* 6 and 11 in Busigny. Two victories were attained by *Jasta* 10 on the 20th and three by *Jastas* 4 and 11 on the 31st.

Fortunately, another proven pilot in the form of Ltn d R Ulrich Neckel was brought in from *Jasta* 12 on 1 September to take command of *Jasta* 6. The 20-year-old already had 24 victories to his name, and had risen rapidly through the ranks at JG II. Neckel would add six more kills with *Jasta* 6, and earn one of the war's last *Pour le Mérite* awards.

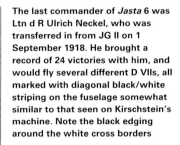

On 4 September, one of Neckel's pilots, Richard Wenzl, was chasing two SE 5s with his *Staffel* mates when they were jumped by Camels from No 46 Sqn. Wenzl claimed his seventh victory;

'At 300 metres, from underneath, I got a hold of a "Tommy" who was attacking one of my comrades. I finally got him in my line of fire to where he had to go spinning down under me. At this point, having fought for a good 15 minutes, I forced him to land near Raillencourt. He set his machine down flawlessly, but then he tried to set it afire. I threatened him with machine gun fire and he desisted.'

Wenzl had shot down Camel B5434 of No 46 Sqn, flown by Lt C Killick, who was taken prisoner.

FINAL DAYS

'Toward the end of the month', Bodenschatz wrote, 'the *Jagdgeschwader* Richthofen is sent to Metz when the Americans attempt a breakthrough there. When it arrives there in the course of 21 and 22 September, *Jagdgeschwader* II had already taken care of everything.'

It took JG I several days to make the arduous move to Metz-Frescaty airfield, in the jurisdiction of *Armee Abteilung C,* but by the 25th they were

The last commander of *Jasta* 6 was Ltn d R Ulrich Neckel, who was transferred in from JG II on 1 September 1918. He brought a record of 24 victories with him, and would fly several different D VIIs, all marked with diagonal black/white striping on the fuselage somewhat similar to that seen on Kirschstein's machine. Note the black edging around the white cross borders

Ltn Schliewen of *Jasta* 6 was a Bavarian, as shown by the barely-visible band of blue and white diamonds just aft of him. Again, the serial number of this D VII (OAW) is obscured. Schliewen is thought to have scored two victories (*HAC/UTD*)

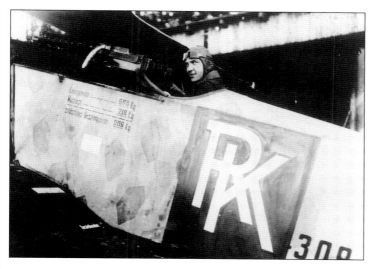

On 26 September Udet attained his final two victories and Ltn d R Richard Kraut of *Jasta* 4 scored his first (and only) success. Kraut was flying BMW D VII (F) 4309/18, seen here at Metz-Frescaty. His *RK* emblem was painted on a dark panel, and the nose, wheels and struts were finished in *Jasta* 4 black. Later, black 'borders' were painted on the fuselage longeron positions, as was common on *Jasta* 4 Fokkers. In late October Kraut was transferred to *Jasta* 63, where his flew Fokker D VII (Alb) 5324/18, which also bore his *RK* marking

Ltn d R Karl 'Carlos' Meyer poses in the cockpit of his D VII (OAW) of *Jasta* 4, which was marked with his chained bulldog emblem. The black borders on the longeron positions were popular in *Jasta* 4, and these would later have white borders added. After the war, Meyer returned to his native Venezuela and was instrumental in the development of military aviation in the country

making orientation flights, and Grassmann of *Jasta* 10 flamed a balloon for his sixth kill. However, JG II had taken a fierce toll of the Americans, and pickings were slim.

On that same 25 September another veteran arrived at *Jasta* 6 to bolster its performance. A native of the Hanseatic city of Bremen, Ltn d R Friedrich Noltenius had 13 victories to his name, earned in *Jasta* 27. Upon his arrival he wrote, 'The Front was perfectly quiet. During the first two days there was no flying activity at all. The *Staffel* had been equipped with new machines – all BMW-Fokkers – which had yet to be assembled'.

Newly-promoted Oblt d R Udet also showed up, and on the 26th he made his final two entries in his record book. His comrades complained that there had been practically no enemy aerial activity in four weeks, yet Udet had aircraft practically drop into his lap after returning from leave. He claimed two de Havilland bombers, and his *Jasta* 4 comrades added two more – however, these claims were contested by *Jasta* 77b, and some sources state *Kofl* 19 gave the credit to the latter unit. Nonetheless, the four bombers are listed in the *Geschwader* diary, and Udet is generally credited with 62 victories. He received a bullet graze wound on his thigh in this fight and went on a short recuperative leave. Although he would return in less than two weeks, Udet did not score again.

Day after day in this period, the war diary reports little enemy activity. On 6 October, Noltenius noted that a French kite balloon was up for the first time. Flying his D VII 5056/18, marked with his fuselage band in the red and white Hanseatic colours, he went after the balloon in a meticulously planned attack;

'Only when I began to dive did the machine guns on the ground start firing. At a distance of 300 metres I started to fire. When I had closed to

Mechanics of *Jasta* 4 pose one mascot of the unit alongside another painted on the side of Karl Meyer's D VII (OAW). This aircraft bore the *Jasta* 4 markings of black nose, struts and wheel covers, and had the commonly applied black and white borders to the fuselage. Note that the cross has been converted from an earlier, thicker style. This D VII was covered in four-colour fabric

100 metres, the balloon was already burning. I made for home at once – the enemy flak started firing too late, and they shot inaccurately as well.'

Although a few skilled performers like Neckel, Noltenius and Laumann could still achieve significant aerial victories against the inexperienced Americans, they could do nothing to slow the inexorable Allied advances. On 9 October the *Geschwader* was moved yet again, this time to Marville, on the Argonne Front. The next day Fokkers of *Jasta* 10 clashed with SPADs of the American First Pursuit Group. Ltns Grassmann and Heldmann each claimed one of the Yanks, but minutes later Ltn Kohlbach was either rammed by, or collided with, the SPAD flown by Lt Wilbert White of the 147th Aero Squadron. Kohlbach was able to safely take to his parachute, but White, a father of two, was killed.

Apparently Kohlbach's falling Fokker was credited to future ranking American ace Capt E V 'Eddie' Rickenbacker of the 94th Aero Squadron, and Kohlbach received credit for White's SPAD.

Most of October yielded little in the way of opponents or combat, but on the 23rd Noltenius, now in *Jasta* 11, was able to enhance the reputation of the *Geschwader,* and his own, by flaming two balloons and a SPAD, to which Ulrich Neckel added another SPAD. Four more victories came on the 29th, at the cost of one novice *Jasta* 6 pilot.

The last kills were claimed in early November, although certainly the airmen could by then read the writing on the wall. On 3 November, it might have seemed like old times for Wenzl, Noltenius and Gussmann, as they contributed to the total of eight aircraft for the day, having Maushake of *Jasta* 4 badly wounded in return. The next day *Jasta* 11 newcomer Ltn

On 9 October 1918 JG I made its penultimate move, this time to Marville in the 5. *Armee* sector. One of Ulrich Neckel's striped Fokker-built D VIIs sits alone on the Marville airfield in this view – perhaps one of the last wartime photographs taken of a JG I aircraft. On 7 November the Wing made its last wartime move to Tellancourt, flying through a pouring rain storm at tree-top level. By then, however, their war was over (*HAC/UTD*)

Oberleutnant Udet with 60 Air Conquests

Alfred Niemz contributed his fourth kill to the bag of four for the wing. Old traditions still held, as Niemz flew a BMW Fokker with a red nose and tail and white arrow painted lengthwise on the lozenge fabric fuselage.

The final day of aerial combat for the legendary Richthofen *Geschwader* occurred on 6 November, when Ltns Grassman, Heldmann and Neckel each claimed a SPAD. According to the *Geschwader* record books, these were the final contributions to the wartime triumphs of JG I. The group made one more retreat, through a drenching rain, to the muddy field at Tellancourt on 7 November. Many aircraft were damaged in landing on the 'soft' and saturated ground, but it hardly mattered. The next day, Neckel became the last JG I pilot to receive the 'Blue Max'. No more such awards would be made, as on the 9th the Kaiser abdicated and fled to the Netherlands. Göring began planning the unit's retreat to the Fatherland.

On 11 November 1918, the embittered pilots flew their Fokkers to Darmstadt. Having been ordered to deliver their aircraft to French authorities at Strasbourg, many of the JG I airmen touched down with less-than-perfect landings at Darmstadt or Strasbourg, damaging most of their machines. The *Geschwader* was demobilised in Aschaffenburg on 19 November. Göring's final statement claimed that *Jagdgeschwader Freiherr von Richthofen* Nr I had accounted for 644 Allied aircraft and lost 56 officers and six enlisted men killed, and 52 officers and seven enlisted men wounded. However, a better epitaph for the young airmen of JG I was perhaps provided by Bodenschatz;

'Together, they were an élite. They learned to fight in a manner unheard of, and they learned to die in a manner unprecedented.'

Udet apparently returned to JG I at Metz on 3 October, bringing with him his famous Siemens Schuckert Werke D III – this was most likely D.8350/17, which had a Siemens-Halske Sh.3a engine built under licence by Rhemag in Mannheim. Udet had the fuselage, struts and wheel covers painted red (the rudder remained white), and this machine became the subject of many publicity photos. The *LO!* emblem was painted only on the starboard side of the fuselage. Udet gave some brilliant flying displays in this aircraft, but scored no victories with it. Friedrich Noltenius of *Jasta* 6 wrote on 6 October, 'I had a little mock dogfight with Udet, who flew the Siemens D III with the powerful Remag (sic) engine that he had brought with him upon returning from leave after being wounded in September. It was impossible to match the performance of this combination'. Nonetheless, the extent of combat flying Udet did with the type remains unknown

Ltn d R Richard Kraut arrived at *Jasta* 4 from *Jastaschule* I on 3 August 1918. When interviewed by Alex Imrie, Kraut said that as a new man, he was assigned one of the oldest D VIIs on hand, a former *Jasta* 6 Fokker-built example. The *Jasta* 6 markings on its nose and tail were painted over with a somewhat translucent coat of black, but the former tail stripes still showed through. Kraut's personal marking on the streaky camouflaged fuselage was a shield of the order of the Teutonic Knights, which was associated with his home city of Thorn, in West Prussia. The captured SPAD VII from SPA62 in the background is probably the machine flown by Udet, who is recorded as having such an aircraft for personal transport. It still bore its French *escadrille* emblem on the side, and the words *Gute Leute* (good people) were painted on the top wing to prevent attacks by other German pilots

APPENDICES

APPENDIX 1

JAGDGESCHWADER Nr I COMMANDERS

Commander	Dates of Command	Notes
Rittm Manfred von Richthofen	26/7/17 to 21/4/18	KIA 21/4/18
Hptm Wilhelm Reinhard	22/4/18 to 3/7/18	Killed in flying accident 3/7/18
Oblt Hermann Göring	8/7/18 to End of War	Died by suicide 15/10/46

APPENDIX 2

JAGDGESCHWADER Nr I *JASTA* COMMANDERS

Commander	Dates of Command	Notes
Jasta 4		
Oblt Kurt von Döring	24/6/17 to 6/7/17	CO JG I, stv
Oblt Oskar von Boenigk	6/7/17 to 25/7/17	stv
Oblt Kurt von Döring	25/7/17 to 6/9/17	CO JG I, stv
Oblt Oskar von Boenigk	6/9/17 to 23/10/17	stv
Oblt Kurt von Döring	23/10/17 to 12/12/17	CO JG I, stv
Ltn d R Kurt Wüsthoff	12/12/17 to 20/12/17	stv
Oblt Kurt von Döring	20/12/17 to 19/1/18	
Ltn d R Kurt Wüsthoff	19/1/18 to 16/3/18	to JG I staff
Ltn H G von der Osten	16/3/18 to 28/3/18	WIA
Ltn d R Johann Janzen	28/3/18 to 3/5/18	PoW
Ltn Viktor von Rautter	4/5/18 to 20/5/18	stv
Ltn d R Ernst Udet	20/5/18 to 14/8/18	JG I
Ltn d R Egon Koepsch	14/8/18 to 19/9/18	stv
Oblt d R Ernst Udet	19/9/18 to 22/10/18	Leave
Ltnd R Heinrich Maushake	22/10/18 to 3/11/18	WIA, stv
Ltn d R Egon Koepsch	3/11/18 to 11/11/18	stv, to end of war
Jasta 6		
Oblt Eduard Dostler	24/6/17 to 21/8/17	KIA
Ltn d L Hans Adam	22/8/17 to 15/11/17	KIA
Oblt Wilhelm Reinhard	16/11/17 to 22/4/18	to CO *JG* I
Ltn d R Johann Janzen	28/4/18 to 9/6/18	PoW
Ltn d R Hans Kirschstein	10/6/18 to 16/7/18	injured in crash*
Ltn d R Paul Wenzel	19/7/18 to 11/8/18	WIA, stv
Ltn d R Richard Wenzl	11/8/18 to 1/9/18	stv
Ltn d R Ulrich Neckel	1/9/18 to 11/11/18	to end of war

* Injured in crash of two-seater, died same day

Commander	Dates of Command	Notes
Jasta 10		
Ltn d R Albert Dossenbach	24/6/17 to 3/7/17	KIA
Oblt Ernst Frhr von Althaus	6/7/17 to 30/7/17	to _Jastaschule_ II
Ltn d R Werner Voss	30/7/17 to 23/9/17	KIA
Oblt Ernst Weigand	24/9/17 to 25/9/17	KIA
Ltn Max Kühn	26/9/17 to 27/9/17	stv
Ltn d R Hans Klein	27/9/17 to 19/2/18	WIA
Ltn d R Hans Weiss	27/3/18 to 1/4/18	stv
Ltn Erich Löwenhardt	1/4/18 to 10/4/18	stv
Ltn Erich Löwenhardt	10/4/18 to 19/6/18	JG I CO, stv
Ltn d R Aloys Heldmann	19/6/18 to 6/7/18	stv
Ltn Erich Löwenhardt	6/7/18 to 10/8/18	KIA
Ltn d R Aloys Heldmann	10/8/18 to 14/8/18	stv
Ltn d R Arthur Laumann	14/8/18 to 11/11/18	to end of war
Jasta 11		
Ltn Karl Allmenröder	24/6/17 to 27/6/17	KIA
Ltn Kurt Wolff	28/6/17 to 11/7/17	WIA
Oblt Wilhelm Reinhard	12/7/17 to 4/8/17	WIA
Ltn Gisbert-Wilhelm Groos	6/9/17 to 11/9/17	stv
Oblt Kurt Wolff	11/9/17 to 15/9/17	KIA
Ltn Gisbert-Wilhelm Groos	16/9/17 to 25/9/17	Hospitalised
Ltn Lothar von Richthofen	25/9/17 to 19/1/18	Leave
Ltn Hans-Georg von der Osten	19/1/18 to 16/2/18	stv
Ltn Lothar von Richthofen	16/2/18 to 13/3/18	WIA
Ltn von Breiten-Landenberg	16/3/18 to 25/3/18	stv
Ltn d R Ernst Udet	25/3/18 to 8/4/18	stv
Ltn d R Hans Weiss	8/4/18 to 2/5/18	stv, KIA
Ltn Eberhard Mohnicke	2/5/18 to 19/7/18	stv
Ltn Lothar von Richthofen	19/7/18 to 26/7/18	JG I CO, stv
Ltn Erich R von Wedel	26/7/18 to 14/8/18	stv
Ltn Eberhard Mohnicke	14/8/18 to 26/8/18	stv
Ltn Wolfram von Richthofen	26/8/18 to 30/8/18	stv
Ltn Erich R von Wedel	31/8/18 to 2/9/18	stv
Ltn Mohnicke	2/9/18 to 4/9/18	stv
Oblt Erich R von Wedel	4/9/18 to 8/9/18	stv
Oblt Erich R von Wedel	8/9/18 to 22/10/18	JG I CO, _stv_
Ltn d R Egon Koepsch	22/10/18 to 4/11/18	
Oblt Erich R von Wedel	4/11/18 to 11/11/18	to end of war

Those who were temporary acting commanders are noted as stv (stellvertreter)

APPENDIX 3

JAGDGESCHWADER Nr I ACES WHO RECEIVED THE *ORDEN POUR LE MÉRITE*

Recipient	JG I Unit(s)	Date of Award	Total Victories
Oblt Ernst von Althaus*	*Jasta* 10	21/7/16	9
Ltn d R Albert Dossenbach*	*Jasta* 10	11/11/16	15
Rittm Manfred von Richthofen	JG I	12/1/17	80
Ltn d R Werner Voss*	*Jasta* 10	8/4/17	48
Oblt Kurt Wolff	*Jasta* 11	4/5/17	33
Ltn Lothar von Richthofen	*Jasta* 11	14/5/17	40
Ltn Karl Allmenröder	*Jasta* 11	14/6/17	30
Oblt Eduard von Dostler	*Jasta* 6	6/8/17	26
Ltn d R Kurt Wüsthoff	*Jasta* 4	22/11/17	26
Oblt d R Hans Klein	*Jastas* 4,10	4/12/17	22
Oblt d R Ernst Udet	*Jastas* 11,4	9/4/18	62
Oblt Erich Löwenhardt	*Jasta* 10	31/5/18	53/54
Oblt Hermann Göring*	JG I	2/6/18	22
Ltn d R Hans Kirschstein	*Jasta* 6	24/6/18	27
Oblt Oskar von Boenigk*	*Jasta* 4	25/10/18	26
Ltn d R Arthur Laumann	*Jasta* 10	25/10/18	27
Ltn d R Ulrich Neckel	*Jasta* 6	8/11/18	30

* Did not win the *Pour le Mérite* during their service in a JG I unit. The first seven names on this list received the Order before JG I was formed

APPENDIX 4

NOTES ON SELECTED *JAGDGESCHWADER* Nr I AIRCRAFT SERIAL NUMBERS

Aircraft	Pilot (if known)	Details
Jagdstaffel 4		
Albatros D V 1162/17	*Vfw* Ernst Clausnitzer	PoW 16/7/17
Pfalz D III 4042/17	*Ltn d R* Skauraudzun	WIA 8/3/18
Pfalz D III 1396/17	*Oblt* Oskar von Boenigk	circa Oct 1917
Albatros D V 4566/17	*Ltn d R* von der Osten(?)	
Fokker Dr I 546/17	*Ltn* Feodor Hübener	PoW 16/5/18
Fokker Dr I 586/17	*Ltn d R* Ernst Udet	formerly Kirschstein's, J 6
Fokker Dr I 593/17	*Ltn d R* Ernst Udet	June/July 1918
Fokker D VII (F) 4253/18	*Ltn d R* Ernst Udet	flown from 29/6/18 onwards
Fokker D VII (F) 378/18		July 1918
Fokker D VII (OAW) 2063/18	*Ltn d R* Julius Bender	parachute jump 16/7/18
Fokker D VII (F) 4275/18		circa Sept 1918
Fokker D VII (F) 4309/18	*Ltn d R* Richard Kraut	Sept 1918
Fokker D VII (F) 4330/18		Oct 1918
Siemens Schuckert D III 8350/17	*Oblt d R* Ernst Udet	Oct 1918
Jagdstaffel 6		
Albatros D V 1148/17	*Ltn d L* Hans Adam	crashed 2/8/17
Albatros D V 1171/17(?)	*Ltn d R* Robert Tüxen	circa July 1917
Albatros D Va 5237/17		Winter 1917
Fokker Dr I 525/17	*Rittm* von Richthofen (JG I)	flown on 17/3/18
Fokker Dr I 556/17	*Ltn d R* Ludwig Beckmann	circa Feb 1918
Fokker Dr I 595/17	*Ltn d R* Franz Hemer	circa March 1918
Fokker Dr I 568/17(?)	*Ltn d R* Robert Tüxen	circa March 1918
Fokker Dr I 586/17	*Ltn d R* Hans Kirschstein	circa May 1918
Fokker E V 148/18		Aug 1918
Fokker E V 153/18	*Ltn d R* Richard Wenzl	Aug 1918
Fokker E V 154/18		Aug 1918
Fokker E V 152/18	*Uffz* Hans Reimers(?)	Aug 1918
Fokker E V 157/18	*Gefr* Kurt Blümener(?)	Aug 1918
Fokker D VII 5056/18	*Ltn d R* Friedrich Noltenius	10/10/18, 15th victory
Jagdstaffel 10		
Fokker F I 103/17	*Ltn d R* Werner Voss	KIA 23/9/17
Pfalz D III 1395/17	*Ltn* Aloys Heldmann	circa Oct 1917
Pfalz D IIIa 8169/17	*Ltn d R* Gustav Bellen	WIA 11/10/17
Pfalz D III 4117/17	*Ltn* Aloys Heldmann	29/11/17, 3rd victory
Pfalz D III 4116/17	*Ltn d R* Friedrich Demandt	KIA 30/11/17
Pfalz D III 1370/17	*Vfw* Hecht	PoW 27/12/17
Pfalz D III 4059/17	*Flg* Hellmuth Riensberg	KIA 18/1/18
Albatros D V 4565/17	*Vfw* Adam Barth	KIA 30/1/18
Pfalz D IIIa 4283/17	*Ltn d R* Hans Klein	WIA 19/2/18
Albatros D Va 5401/17	*Ltn* Aloys Heldmann	9/3/18, 4th victory
Albatros D V 4571/17	*Ltn d R* Franz Bohlein	crashed March 1918
Fokker D VII 234/18	*Ltn* 'Fritz' Friedrichs	circa May 1918
Fokker D VII 244/18	*Ltn d R* Heldmann	23/6/18, 7th victory

Aircraft	Pilot (if known)	Details
***Jagdstaffel* 10 (continued)**		
Fokker D VII 309/18	*Ltn d R* 'Fritz' Friedrichs	KIA 15/7/18*
Fokker D VII (F) 4264/18	*Ltn d R* Aloys Heldmann	circa August 1918

* Failed parachute jump when ammunition self-ignited

Aircraft	Pilot (if known)	Details
***Jagdstaffel* 11**		
Albatros D V 1177/17	*Rittm* von Richthofen	June/July 1917
Albatros D V 2059/17	*Rittm* von Richthofen	August 1917
Albatros D V 2161/17	*Ltn* von Linsingen	circa July 1917
Fokker F I 102/17	Richthofen/Kurt Wolff	Wolff KIA 15/9/17
Fokker Dr I 113/17	*Vfw* Lautenschlager	KIA 29/10/17
Fokker Dr I 121/17	*Ltn* Günther Pastor	wing failure 31/10/17
Albatros D V 4693/17	*Rittm* von Richthofen	November 1917
Albatros D V 4628/17	*Ltn* Siegfried Gussmann	destroyed 4/12/17
Albatros D Va 5313/17	*Ltn* Traugott von Schweinitz	destroyed 27/12/18
Pfalz D IIIa 4223/17	*Ltn* von Linsingen	crashed 24/1/18
Fokker Dr I 144/17	*Ltn* Eberhard Stapenhorst	PoW 13/1/18
Fokker Dr I 155/17	*Ltn* Hans Joachim Wolff	wing damage 3/2/18
Fokker Dr I 161/17	*Rittm* von Richthofen	March 1918
Fokker Dr I 110/17	*Ltn* Erich Just	WIA 1/3/18
Fokker Dr I 106/17	*Ltn d R* Erich Bahr	KIA 6/3/18
Fokker Dr I 147/17	*Ltn* Keseling (*Jasta* 10)	PoW 24/3/18
Fokker Dr I 152/17	*Rittm* von Richthofen	March 1918
Fokker Dr I 454/17	*Ltn* Lothar von Richthofen	13/3/18, injured
Fokker Dr I 149/17	*Ltn d R* Ernst Udet	28/3/18
Fokker Dr I 477/17	*Rittm* von Richthofen	March/April 1918
Fokker Dr I 163/17	*Ltn* v Linsingen/von Conta	Feb/March 1918
Fokker Dr I 425/17	*Rittm* von Richthofen	KIA 21/4/18
Fokker Dr I 564/17	*Ltn* Werner Steinäuser	April 1918
Fokker Dr I 545/17	*Ltn* Hans Weiss	KIA 2/5/18
Fokker Dr I 591/17	*Vfw* Edgar Scholz (Scholtz)	KIA 2/5/18
Fokker D VII (F) 294/18	*Oblt* Hermann Göring	18/7/18, 22nd victory
Fokker D VII (F) 377/18		August 1918
Fokker D VII (F) 325/18		August 1918
Fokker D VII 286/18	*Vfw* Willi Gabriel	circa June 1918
Fokker D VII (F) 5125/18	*Oblt* Hermann Göring	Oct 1918

COLOUR PLATES

All of the artwork in this section has been created by Harry Dempsey, who has worked closely with the author in an effort to illustrate the aircraft as accurately as possible, given the limited information available. The colours portrayed are approximations only, and are sometimes purely assumptions. The ground breaking research of historian Alex Imrie provided inspiration and made much of this artwork possible. The works of A E Ferko, William Puglisi, Bruno Schmäling and H D Hastings were also very beneficial. The research and kind advice of Manfred Thiemeyer was extremely valuable, as was the assistance of Ray Rimell, Dan-San Abbott, Geoff Schroder, Jörn Leckschied, Alan Toelle and Bob English. The responsibility for the opinions expressed is the author's alone.

1
Albatros D III (serial unknown) of Rittm Manfred von Richthofen, *Jasta* 11, Roucourt, April 1917
This famous D III appears in several photographs, but its serial number is still a mystery – the centrally-mounted radiator in the wing reveals that it could not have been D. 789/17, which Richthofen flew in June. It was this D III that began the 'red battle flier' legend, and the fuselage, struts, wheel covers and entire tail was painted in red. The insignia on the fuselage and tail were subdued with a thin coat of red as well. Note the small unpainted rectangle on the clear-doped fabric fin, which left the Albatros company crest untouched. The wings retained factory camouflage of Venetian Red (chestnut brown), olive green and a light Brunswick green, with the undersides in light blue.

2
Albatros D V (serial unknown) of Ltn d R Franz Müller, *Jasta* 11, Marckebeeke, July 1917
This D V illustrates the standard form of unit marking adopted by *Jasta* 11 in the summer of 1917, which was comprised of a red nose back to the cockpit, as well as red struts and wheel covers. The tail surfaces were painted a personal colour – in this case white – with additional green and white fuselage decoration. The green colour was extended to obscure the white fuselage cross border in *Jasta* 11 fashion. The painted wing camouflage now consisted of lilac and green shades, with light blue undersides.

3
Albatros D V (serial unknown) of Ltn Carl August von Schönebeck, *Jasta* 11, Marckebeeke, August 1917
This illustration is provisional, and is based on a description von Schönebeck gave to Jon Guttman in 1981, as well as on *Jasta* 11 marking practices. It displayed the typical unit red colour on the nose, struts and undercarriage, and the pilot's personal lilac colour on the tail. The wings were covered in five-colour lozenge fabric.

4
Albatros D V D.1162/17 of Vfw Ernst Clausnitzer, *Jasta* 4, Marcke, July 1917
Clausnitzer was shot down by 2Lt Langsland of No 23 Sqn RFC on 16 July as he attacked a balloon. His D V became the subject of some scrutiny, and reports indicate it had a 'bright' yellow spinner and a darker yellow tail – both part of the pilot's personal marking. The black spiral ribbon around the plywood fuselage was the *Jasta* 4 unit marking. Metal cowling panels and struts were finished in a dull grey or greyish-green, and the wings were probably in green and lilac ('mauve') camouflage on uppersurfaces and light blue on the undersides.

5
Albatros D V (serial unknown) of Ltn d R Kurt Wüsthoff, *Jasta* 4, Lieu St Amand, February 1918
The attribution of this aircraft to Wüsthoff is provisional, but the tail décor and *W* certainly argue in favour of it. It is presumed that the tail and wheel cover markings were in black and white, and the *W* was black as well (although it did extend over the black ribbon *Jasta* marking in places). The spinner marking is assumed, based on Wüsthoff's earlier D III. The wings would have been camouflaged in shades of green and lilac, with all metal cowling panels a dull grey or greyish-green.

6
Albatros D V (serial and pilot unknown), *Jasta* 4, Marcke, circa August 1917
Much of this description is assumed. This D V displayed a slightly thicker version of the *Jasta* marking ribbon. The personal marking consisted of the polka-dot-decorated tail and spinner, the colours of which are entirely speculative – black, red or other dark colours are possible. The wings were covered in five-colour printed camouflage fabric.

7
Albatros D V D.1177/17 of Rittm Manfred Freiherr von Richthofen, JG I, Marckebeeke, June 1917
Based on the photos taken at Gontrode and on Richthofen's combat reports, this aircraft is thought to have been red overall. The wings were given a somewhat translucent coat of red, through which the camouflage pattern and crosses could still be discerned. The serial number is derived from the combat reports.

8
Albatros D V D.1148/17 of Ltn Hans Adam, *Jasta* 6, Bisseghem, August 1917
Adam wrote off this aircraft while landing on 2 August, but remained unhurt. The D V was marked with black/white *Jasta* 6 décor on the tailplane and adjacent fuselage, and the stripes were repeated beneath the lower wings as well. In addition, it bore a white-bordered fuselage band assumed to have been black. The nose was also painted a dark colour, interpreted as black. The wings probably bore painted lilac and green camouflage, with light blue undersides.

9
Albatros D V D.1171/17(?) of Ltn d R Robert Tüxen, *Jasta* 6, Bisseghem, July 1917
The serial number quoted here is very provisional, based on the one hazy photograph which shows the fin. This D V displayed the classic 'zebra' stripes of *Jasta* 6 on its tail

and also beneath the lower wings. Tüxen's personal emblem was the thinly-applied white band around the fuselage. Metal cowling panels appear rather dark, being perhaps a dull greyish-green in colour. The wings were camouflaged in green and lilac, while the rudder was covered in clear-doped fabric.

10
Albatros D Va D.5237/17, pilot unknown, *Jasta* 6, Lieu St Amand, December 1917
Much about this D Va is speculative, but the markings and serial number seem to indicate that it was a *Jasta* 6 aircraft from the early winter of 1917-18. The usual *Jasta* 6 décor appeared on the tail surfaces, and the pilot's personal marking was a black(?) and white fuselage band applied in the *Staffel* manner. The wings and rudder were covered in five-colour lozenge fabric, with metal cowling panels a dull grey.

11
Albatros D III (serial unknown) of Vfw Ernst Günther Burggaller, *Jasta* 10, Marcke, September 1917
The photographs of this aircraft came from the late Heinz Nowarra, who corresponded with mechanic Xaver Leinmüller and other *Jasta* 10 members. The D III is generally recorded as having been flown by Burggaller. However, it has also been attributed to Gustav Bellen. Leinmüller served às mechanic for both Burggaller and Bellen, and it is possible that both pilots flew this D III. It bore the usual *Jasta* 10 yellow nose and a white fuselage bar as personal emblem (along with the black numeral '7'). Wheel covers may have been yellow/white or black/white. Most unusual are the small auxiliary struts affixed to the interplane struts, and a headrest which must have been fitted at *Jasta* 10. The wings and tailplane were camouflaged in Venetian red, olive green and light Brunswick green, with a clear-doped fabric rudder.

12
Albatros D III (OAW) of Ltn Erich Löwenhardt, *Jasta* 10, Marcke, September 1917
Nowarra also identified this aircraft as the machine flown by Löwenhardt, again presumably based on statements from Leinmüller or fellow *Jasta* 10 mechanic, Georg Junginger. It was decided this attribution was reliable enough to quote here. This D III had a white wavy 'snake-line' applied to the fuselage sides and the top surface of the upper wing as well. The standard *Jasta* 10 nose colour was displayed, as well as a small personal number '15'. Being an OAW product, the wings may have been camouflaged in lilac and green, but chestnut brown and one or two shades of green camouflage is also possible.

13
Pfalz D III D.1395/17 of Ltn d R Aloys Heldmann, *Jasta* 10, Marcke, September 1917
Some of the early Pfalz from the initial production batch were finished in a terrain camouflage on the uppersurfaces, probably consisting of shades of lilac and green. D III D.1395/17 is shown here as it arrived fresh from the factory, with *silbergrau* (silver-grey) undersides. At some point the wheel covers were painted a very light colour, as seen in the well-known Sanke card Nr 664, and the yellow nose of the *Jasta* may have been added as well.

When interviewed by Jon Guttman in 1981, Heldmann said this Pfalz had a white tail (and wheel covers), and that he later flew a silver Pfalz with a white tail as well. However, notes from his combat reports mention *blue* tail markings on his Pfalz and Albatros fighters, so readers may make up their own minds.

14
Pfalz D III (serial unknown) of Ltn Werner Voss, *Jasta* 10, Marcke, September 1917
Caution is advised in regard to this interpretation. It is based on a very distant photograph that some have stated was Voss' Pfalz D III. It is known that he sometimes flew a Pfalz, but not often. The photo shows two black(?) bands around the fuselage adjacent to the fuselage cross, and the early form of yellow nose marking initially applied to *Jasta* 10 Pfalz. The similarity between these markings and those on Vfw Hecht's D III D.1370/17, captured on 27 December, makes it tempting to suggest that the 'Voss' D III was D.1370/17 in an earlier guise, but this is more speculation.

15
Pfalz D III (serial unknown) of Ltn Hans Klein, *Jasta* 10, Marcke, circa November 1917
As Klein appears in a photograph with this D III, it has been assumed to have been his, but that remains speculative. The lengthwise stripe and over-painted tail *appear* to be the same chrome yellow colour as the nose, struts and wheel covers.

16
Pfalz D III D.1371/17 of Vfw Friedrich Rüdenberg, *Jasta* 10, Marcke, circa October 1917
Rüdenberg, a Jewish pilot who served in JG I, flew this Pfalz D III in September/October 1917. The yellow *Staffel* markings are in evidence, as are Rüdenberg's personal stripe markings on the fuselage and tail surfaces. The black and red colours depicted are entirely provisional. The serial number is partially obscured, but the final two digits are 71, and it seems likely that this was the next in line after Vfw Hecht's D.1370/17, which also went to *Jasta* 10.

17
Pfalz D III D.1396/17 of Oblt Oskar Freiherr von Boenigk, *Jasta* 4, Marckebeeke, circa October 1917
Jasta 4 also received the Pfalz D III, and pilots' personal colours were generally applied on the tail sections. The photo of von Boenigk in this aircraft reveals that about half of the top surface of the lower wing (about four rib spaces adjacent to the fuselage) was painted a 'dark' colour, apparently as an additional identification display. The tail of this D III is not visible in the photo, but the author assumes it was painted in the same colour. It seems likely that it was yellow – the colour of von Boenigk's old unit, the *Grenadier Regiment* Nr 11 *'König Friedrich* III'.

18
Pfalz D IIIa (serial and pilot unknown), *Jasta* 4, Lieu St Amand, circa January 1918
The pilot of this *Jasta* 4 Pfalz D IIIa remains an enigma, but his personal markings consisted of the black chordwise stripes on the elevator and fin. These were probably applied to the horizontal stabiliser as well.

19
Fokker Dr I 127/17 of Rittm Manfred von Richthofen, JG I, Léchelle, March 1918
This Dr I appears in two *Jasta* 11 line-up photos. The pattern of streaking on the wings and fuselage and the worn and flaking paint on the insignia on the rudder are all consistent with earlier photos of 127/17 before the red décor was completed. Richthofen's combat reports (victories 71, 74 and 76) describe the markings as shown in the photos. Red was applied to the upper decking of the fuselage as well as the tail and top wing. The olive paint used to alter the cross fields on the fuselage and rudder was apparently of poor quality, and much of that paint has worn away. If any red was used over the crossfield on the fuselage, it too may have flaked away before the photos were taken.

20
Fokker Dr I (possibly 155/17) of Ltn Eberhardt Mohnicke, *Jasta* 11, Léchelle, March 1918
Mohnicke had previously flown in *Kagohl* 2, and had brought the swastika marking with him from that unit. The fuselage aft of the cockpit was a very pale colour (here shown as blue), and standard *Jasta* 11 red markings were applied. Mohnicke was wounded on 1 March in Dr I 155/17, which may have been this aircraft. The war diary says his machine was undamaged. This swastika-marked machine stayed in the unit until late April at least, when it bore early *Balkenkreuz* insignia and a white rudder and was flown by someone else after Mohnicke.

21
Fokker Dr I (serial and pilot unknown), *Jasta* 11, Léchelle, March 1918
Seen in the same line-up photo as Richthofen's Dr I 127/17, this interesting triplane remains unidentified. It bore tail stripes similar (but not identical) to those seen on Dr I 502/17 in the well-known Léchelle line-up photograph. The stripes are provisionally depicted as black and white, but other interpretations are possible. Standard *Jasta* 11 markings were seen.

22
Fokker Dr I (serial unknown) of Ltn Hans Joachim Wolff, Léchelle, March 1918
Yellow was the colour of Wolff's former unit, *Schleswig-Holsteinisches Ulanen Regt Nr 15*, and this is reflected in his personal fuselage band aft of the cockpit. Again, typical *Jasta* 11 markings are in place. The serial number is unknown, but Wolff was flying Dr I 155/17 when it suffered wing failure on 3 February 1918.

23
Fokker Dr I 545/17 of Ltn Hans Weiss, *Jasta* 11, Cappy, April/May 1918
Weiss' personal colour was, appropriately, white, and as a formation leader he had this colour applied to the uppersurface of the top wing, as well as the rear fuselage, tail and upper fuselage decking. Cowling, struts and wheel covers were red. Weiss died in this Dr I on 2 May 1918.

24
Fokker Dr I 564/17 of Ltn Werner Steinhäuser, *Jasta* 11, Cappy, April 1918

Dr I 564/17 was marked with Steinhäuser's personal red and golden yellow colours, which derived from his former regiment. These were displayed as a red *X* on a yellow fuselage bands, and red stripes on a yellow tailplane. These tail stripes *may* have been applied to the fuselage area beneath the tailplane as well, but the photo does not clarify this.

25
Fokker Dr I 556/17, formerly of Ltn Ludwig 'Lutz' Beckmann, *Jasta* 6, Léchelle, March 1918
This Dr I bore the Westphalian red and white fuselage band of 'Lutz' Beckmann, who had served briefly in *Jasta* 6 but had left the unit on 21 February. Even this red/white 'snakeline' marking had been applied over an earlier marking of a lightning bolt, now faded or partially subdued. When photographed at Léchelle in late March, it still bore Beckmann's insignia, and the unit's black cowling and black/white tail stripes.

26
Fokker Dr I 403/17 of Ltn Johann Janzen, *Jasta* 6, Lieu St Amand, circa March 1918
Janzen's Dr I displayed the typical *Jasta* 6 black and white tail stripes and black cowling. The rudder was painted black to produce the white cross edging. The pilot's personal emblem was a white wavy line on a black fuselage band, bordered in white on its leading edge. On 9 May 1918, Janzen survived being shot down in a triplane by Capt O G LeBoutillier of No 209 Sqn. Janzen's rudder cable was shot away, but a strong wing blew him east into marshland near the Somme.

27
Fokker Dr I 586/17 of Ltn d R Ernst Udet, *Jasta* 4, Beugneux-Cramoiselle, June 1918
This flamboyantly painted Dr I was formerly flown by Hans Kirschstein of *Jasta* 6, who decorated it with the diagonal black/white stripes as an 'optical illusion' to confuse the aim of enemy pilots. It was then handed down to *Jasta* 4 when the former unit obtained D VIIs, and Udet flew it in its *Jasta* 6 markings, adding only his *LO!* emblem, probably in red.

28
Fokker D VII (serial unknown) of Offz-Stv Paul Aue, *Jasta* 10, Beugneux, June 1918
An early Fokker-built D VII, this machine bore the streaky factory-applied camouflage on its fuselage and tail, and (probably) four-colour lozenge fabric wings. Aue decorated the fuselage with the coat of arms of his native Saxony. *Jasta* 10 unit markings consisted of the yellow nose, struts and wheel covers.

29
Fokker D VII (OAW) (serial unknown) of Ltn d R Ernst Udet, *Jasta* 4, Bernes, August 1918
Udet flew this machine from Bernes, and it is well-documented in several photos. Covered in four-colour lozenge fabric, it displayed the *Jasta* 4 unit markings of a black nose, struts and wheel covers, as well as the popular *Staffel* touch of outlining the fuselage with black/white borders. Udet's *LO!* emblem appeared on the fuselage, and his usual white chevron leader's tail marking extended

to the trailing edge of the elevators, as seen in the scrap view on page 47.

30

Fokker D VII (OAW) (serial unknown) of Ltn Karl 'Carlos' Meyer, *Jasta* 4, Monthussart Farm, July 1918

Caracas-born Karl Meyer (also known as Carlos Meyer Baldo) flew this D VII from Monthussart Farm, near Braisne, in late July. It bore the usual *Jasta* 4 black markings and the black/white borders on the longeron positions. Meyer's personal emblem was the drooling bulldog on a chain. He achieved four confirmed victories.

31

Fokker D VII of Ltn d R Richard Kraut, *Jasta* 4, Bernes, August 1918

Kraut joined *Jasta* 4 on 3 August, and as a newcomer, he received an old ex-*Jasta* 6 Fokker-built D VII in streaky camouflage, while the rest of the unit had newer OAW-built machines. This scout originally bore *Jasta* 6 markings (as Kraut related to Alex Imrie), which were thinly overpainted in black at *Jasta* 4. Kraut's personal emblem at this time was the shield of the order of the Teutonic Knights, which had founded his home city of Thorn.

32

Fokker D VII (F) 4253/18 of Oblt d R Ernst Udet, *Jasta* 4, Metz-Frescaty, September 1918

Udet flew this aircraft in August and September, and his combat reports for his 46th victory (8 August) and his last two (26 September) both describe its red fuselage and leader's pennants trailing from the elevators. This BMW-powered Fokker may have served in *Jasta* 11, and it is presumed that the nose, struts and wheel covers were red as well (although they might have been *Jasta* 4 black). The style of cowling panels illustrated is provisional, with four-colour lozenge fabric wings.

33

Fokker D VII (serial unknown) of Ltn d R Heinrich 'Heinz' Drekmann, *Jasta* 4, Monthussart Farm, July 1918

Udet wrote that he managed to obtain two BMW-engined Fokkers for *Jasta* 4 at the end of June, and gave the spare to his friend Drekmann, and the two flew many sorties together. It is presumed (but not confirmed) that this D VII seen with Drekmann is that BMW Fokker. Drekmann came from Harburg on the Elbe, part of the Hanseatic League city of Hamburg. The emblem on this D VII was a '*Kogge*' (cog), the type of merchant ship favoured by the early Hanseatic traders, and emblematic of the free cities. The fuselage was obviously painted a very dark colour, which might have been *Jasta* 4 black or even red. The former has been chosen, as it is felt that Drekmann would not have used red as this could have led to confusion with Udet's aircraft. This was to be avoided in order to facilitate confirmation of kills for both men. The type of cowling panels shown is an entirely arbitrary choice, and earlier styles are also possible.

34

Fokker D VII (OAW) of Ltn Schliewen, *Jasta* 6, Bernes, September 1918

This illustration depicts the format of *Jasta* 6 unit markings for Fokker D VIIs. The black/white stripes were applied to the tailplane, nose and even wheel covers. Four-colour fabric covered the airframe, and Schliewen's personal insignia was the black-bordered band of the Bavarian pattern of blue and white diamonds.

35

Fokker E V 157/18 of Gefr Kurt Blümener, *Jasta* 6, Bernes, August 1918

Decked out in the unit markings of *Jasta* 6, this aircraft shows off the black/white *Staffel* colours on its nose, tail and wheel covers. The association with Blümener is very tentative, as 'Wolff III' was also photographed with this machine, and Blümener was photographed in 152/18! The personal marking was a black/white quartering on the four-colour fabric of the fuselage. The finish of the plywood-covered wings is still controversial. Most likely, they were stained and then painted in a somewhat streaky camouflage, resulting in a dark greenish impression.

36

Fokker E V 153/18, Ltn d R Richard Wenzl, *Jasta* 6, Bernes, August 1918

Wenzl was a stalwart JG I veteran, and his *Jasta* 11 Dr I, *Jasta* 6 D VII and this E V all displayed his personal emblem of a black/white fuselage band in the proportions of the Iron Cross medal ribbon, but with the colours reversed. This E V otherwise bore *Jasta* 6 markings.

37

Fokker D VII (serial unknown) of Ltn d R Erich Just, *Jasta* 11, Bernes, August 1918

Much of this illustration, and its attribution to Just, is provisional. This aircraft appears in a line-up of BMW D VIIs in the background of two photographs of a captured Sopwith Camel taken at Bernes. The fuselage sash is identical to the emblem used by Just (see *Osprey Aircraft of the Aces* 53, page 20), and it is tentatively assumed that the line-up shows *Jasta* 11 Fokkers. The tail markings are provisionally depicted after much eye-straining study of the two photos!

38

Fokker D VII (F) 4253/18 of Oblt Hermann Göring, JG I, Metz-Frescaty, October 1918

Previously flown by Udet, this machine was apparently taken over by Göring at some point late in the war. He retained some of the red colouration, but had the rear fuselage repainted in his personal white. The cockpit edge on the port side was cut away and a handle was affixed to the fuselage. The wings were four-colour fabric.

39

Fokker D VII (serial unknown) of Ltn Hans Kirschstein, *Jasta* 6, Beugneux, July 1918

Wenzl described this machine in his book, and now that a partial photo was available (courtesy of Bob English), a provisional illustration begged to be done. This *very* tentative depiction is based on the photo, as well as examination of later, similarly-striped D VIIs flown by Neckel (which did not have painted wings). The diagonal black/white stripes were applied to every possible surface, including the undercarriage 'sub-wing'. Much here is assumed, especially the top surface of the upper wing and the style of crosses shown there. There is no explanation for the single 'thicker' black stripe in the centre of the top wing, unless it was thought to produce even more of an optical illusion (or was it the result of a miscalculation when laying out and painting the stripes?!).

40 (tail scrap view)
Albatros D III D.629/17, Ltn Karl Allmenröder, *Jasta* 11, Roucourt, May 1917
This view of the tail of Ltn Allmenröder's Albatros is intended to illustrate the characteristic style of *Jasta*

markings instituted in mid-April 1917. Many D IIIs had largely red fuselages and tails, with some small trim in another colour for personal identification (see *Osprey Aircraft of the Aces 32 - Albatros Aces of World War 1*).

41 (tail scrap view)
Fokker D VII of Ltn d R Richard Wenzl, *Jasta* 6, Beugneux, June 1918
This view depicts the classic *Jasta* 6 tail markings, which were also applied to Ltn Schliewen's D VII.

BIBLIOGRAPHY

BODENSCHATZ, K, *Jagd in Flanderns Himmel,* Munich, 1935

DUIVEN, R, FRANKS, N, AND BAILEY, F, *The Jasta War Chronology,* London

FERKO, A E, *Richthofen,* Berkhamsted, Herts, 1995

FISCHER, SUZANNE HAYES, *Mother of Eagles - The War Diary of Baroness von Richthofen,* Atglen, PA, 2001 (translation of Kunigunde von Richthofen's *Mein Kriegstagebuch*)

FRANKS, N, BAILEY, F AND DUIVEN, R, *The Jasta Pilots,* London, 1996

FRANKS, N, BAILEY, F AND GUEST, R, *Above the Lines,* London, 1993

FRANKS, N, GIBLIN, H, AND McCRERY, N, *Under the Guns of the Red Baron,* London, 1995

GIBBONS, F, *The Red Knight of Germany,* New York, 1927

GROSZ, P, AND FERKO, A E, 'The Fokker Dr I, A Reappraisal', *Air Enthusiast No 8,* London, 1978

GROSZ, P, *Windsock Datafile 9, Fokker D VII,* Berkhamsted, 1989

HAYZLETT, JAN (TRANSLATOR), *Hunting with Richthofen* (translation of Bodenschatz, *Jagd in Flanderns Himmel*), London, 1996

HENSHAW, T, *The Sky Their Battlefield,* London, 1995

IMRIE, A, *The Fokker Triplane,* London, 1992

IMRIE, A, *Osprey Airwar 17 – German Fighter Units June 1917-1918,* London, 1978

IMRIE, A, *Vintage Warbirds 16 – German Army Air Aces of World War One,* Poole, 1987

ITALIAANDER, R, *Manfred Freiherr von Richthofen,* Berlin, 1938

KILDUFF, P, *Germany's First Air Force,* London, 1991

KILDUFF, P, *The Illustrated Red Baron,* London, 1999

KILDUFF, P, *The Red Baron Combat Wing, Jagdgeschwader Richthofen in Battle,* 1997

KILDUFF, P, *Richthofen, Beyond the Legend of the Red Baron,* New York, 1993

LANGSDORFF, W (ed), *Flieger am Feind,* Gütersloh, circa 1935

NEUMANN, G (ed), *In der Luft unbesiegt,* Munich, 1923

O'CONNOR, N, *Aviation Awards of Imperial Germany in World War I and the Men Who Earned Them,* Vols. 1 to VII, Princeton NJ and Atglen PA, 1988 to 2003

RICHTHOFEN, M, *Der rote Kampfflieger,* Berlin, 1917, and 1935

RIMELL, R (ED), *Fokker D VII Anthology No 1,* Berkhamsted, 1997

UDET, E, *Ace of the Iron Cross,* Garden City, 1970

UDET, E, *Kreuz wider Kokarde,* München, 1918

UDET, E, *Mein Fliegerleben,* Berlin, 1935

VAN ISHOVEN, A (ed. C BOWYER), *The Fall of an Eagle,* London, 1977

WENZL, R, *Richthofen-Flieger,* Freiburg, circa 1930

ZUERL, W, *Pour le Mérite-Flieger,* Munich, 1938

INDEX

References to illustrations are shown in **bold**. Plates are shown with page and caption locators in brackets.